Ghosts and Haunts of Pennsylvania

Shannon Boyer Jones

ISBN: 1478336323
ISBN-13: 9781478336327

DEDICATION

To All Those Who Believe

CONTENTS

Just a Note

Inside this book are many portions of paranormal investigations at various locations. These bits reflect informational pieces, points related to the stories, and just good recordings that were caught. They do not represent all questions asked or various other points of the entire investigation. Keep in mind that during a paranormal investigation many questions will be asked with only a few answers received by the investigator.

ACKNOWLEDGMENTS

I would like to extend a very appreciative thank you to all the members of the Black Moon Paranormal Society; both past and present, for their assistance on investigations and for their contributions to this book. Also, a big thank you to Jason Jones for taking most of the pictures for this book. Finally, of course none of this would have been possible if not for those who have gone before us to make paranormal science and research what it is today.

Cover Photograph: Taken at Valley Forge

"Even in death, the emotions of life remain. Men, women, and children are still individuals, much like how they were in life, they have their own choices and reasons for what they do."

- Shannon Boyer Jones

"It is wonderful that five thousand years have now elapsed since the creation of the world, and still it is undecided whether or not there has ever been an instance of the spirit of any person appearing after death. All argument is against it; but all belief is for it."

- Samuel Johnson, in his autobiography

Investigation Terms and Definitions

Electronic Voice Phenomenon (EVPS) - are voices that are "captured" using a digital recorder or spirit box that have no human source. There are various theories as to how this works and the potential of it. The simple answer is that ghosts and/or spirits often speak on different wave lengths than those of us who are living. If you are using a digital recorder and hear an extra voice in the play back, you may have an EVP.

Electromagnetic Force (EMF) – is when a magnetic field induces an electrical current. This is believed to be connected with paranormal activity.

Spirit Box – is a device that is used by some paranormal investigators in order to gain real time responses when communicating with the deceased. Unlike a digital recorder, this device is, essentially, a modified radio that quickly sweeps through radio stations and produces a high frequency white noise. The trick with these is to listen for responses that occur through several sweeps of radio stations; if the response is on longer than a radio station, and it makes sense to your questions, that is the one you put in your notes to review later.

White Noise – is what many say that ghosts speak through; although this is not always the case. Without getting into all the technical components of what white noise is; think instead about the sound that an amplifier makes before a musical instrument is played. That noise is the sound of white noise.

Introduction

~ Tales can be spun and woven into a web of half-truths, make believe and inventive stories set to scare and fascinate. It is only when the sight is focused on what lies behind the web that a new picture can arise and what was once hidden will become clear never before known to our world. ~

Imagine, if you will, an old three story house with red siding that was built in the 1700s, blocked from the road by two large oak trees. A red brick porch wraps around half the building. Inside, there is a hallway, a staircase, and a choice between: following the staircase to the second floor apartments, a door that leads to the un-renovated first floor that is nothing but log cabin walls and a crumbling old stone fireplace, or a door that leads into the basement where no human has gone in years.

You open the door to the basement, climbing down the creaking wooden steps into the darkness, flicking a light switch to illuminate the ghastly room. Half of the room is urinals, from when the building was used as a bar and tavern; the other half is closed off by stones except for one tiny doorway. Many, many years ago, in that tiny hovel hid escaped slaves; travelers on the Underground Railroad. The tense emotions within that little room: fear, anger, sorrow, hope, not knowing who would be free and who would die in their drastic escape to freedom; all left a plethora of chaotic energy that would last for years.

The light barely penetrates the additional room that is veiled in darkness; but what can be seen is a hole in the stone wall of the foundation, several feet off the ground. The hole is an entrance to a tunnel; one part of which is linked to the basement of the addition that was added on to the house, the other known part leads to the Conewago Creek.

As you stare, the feeling in the room grows tense and the hair on the back of your neck rises. Within the darkness, you see a shadow move. Terrified you run back up the staircase, as you run you hear footsteps running behind you, chasing you to the top. As you reach the first floor, you slam the basement door and continue running to the second floor. The smell of cigar smoke billows down the tiny empty bed room sized apartments of the third floor.

The second floor is only slightly less chilling than the basement. No matter where you go, you feel the eyes watching you. Noises could be heard in the night as the sounds of heavy boots stomp across the floors. While lying in bed at night, the sounds of horses on the stones in the driveway would carry up to the bedroom and a full body apparition in a gray haze would drift through the bedroom. In your dreams, the ghost of an escaped slave would appear and pointing towards the old bridge that ran across the creek and warns you to stay away from the windows and beware the lanterns in the night. All the while, the family dog would bark sporadically at invisible entities in the remodeled kitchen in the apartment.

This is how I lived for a year of my teens. It was extremely frightening at times and caused me to back away from the "true" ghost stories that I used to love to read as a kid. I was always a believer, but it is a horse of a different color when you learn firsthand that ghosts are real and can infiltrate your life. I tolerated living in that place as well as I could but; it was not until a few years later that I was able to gather my courage to begin exploring haunted locations again. I realized that my time in that house showed me that the living are not the only ones in need of help and to be heard; though the paranormal can be frightening, it is only a few of those spirits that do mean harm. Ghosts are, after all, still people. Death does not have to mean loneliness if the living are willing to listen.

Perhaps together, we can help these souls find rest and peace in their afterlives; and write a new history of the world.

Shannon Boyer Jones

HISTORICAL FACTS TIMELINE

Before 1638- Only Native Americans inhabited the area.

1600s

1638 – Swedish made the first permanent settlement in the state.

1647 – Dutch set up a trading post.

1655- Dutch took the land from the Swedish.

1664- English took the land from the Dutch.

1673-1674- Dutch fought to retake control of the land from the English. [1]

1681- King Charles II grants land in what would become known as Pennsylvania to William Penn and his family in honor of Penn's father Admiral Sir William Penn. The Penn family then beings the task of paying the Native American inhabitants for their land claims. This was done before Penn, his family, and their Quaker followers began inhabiting the land and giving grants.

Over the years: Germans, Scotch-Irish, African Americans and; to a lesser extent, French Huguenots, Jewish, Irish, and Welsh settlers would come to the state.

1700s

---

[1] "Pennsylvania on the Eve of Colonization." *Pennsylvania General Assembly.* 1 Jan. 2011. Web. 1 May 2011.
<www.legis.state.pa.us/wu01/vc/visitor_info/pa_history/pa_history.htm>.

1755- July 9th – the event known as Braddock's Defeat occurred near what is now modern day Pittsburgh. British and American troops were attacked and defeated by Native Americans and their French allies.

1756-1763 - The French and Indian War

1756 – Forts are built all along the Susquehanna River for the French and Indian War; among the forts built: Fort Halifax (Dauphin Co.), Fort Hunter (Dauphin Co.), and Fort Duquesne (Allegheny Co.).

1757 – Fort Halifax is dismantled and its garrison is moved to Fort Hunter. [2]

1758 – Members of a Shawnee tribe and a few Frenchmen attack the Jemison family farm near modern day Chambersburg. Five members of the family were killed in the attack and a sixth member, Mary, was kidnapped and adopted by a Seneca family.

1763 – 1766 – Pontiac's Rebellion – Ottawa Chief Pontiac leads a rebellion against the British. Military conflicts began in 1763 and ended in 1764; a formal treaty was not drawn until 1766.

1763 – August 1st – Battle of Bushy Run. [3]

The American Revolution

1768 – By this year, the Penn family had purchased all but the Northwestern third part of the state from the Native American inhabitants.

1771- Fort Mifflin (Philadelphia Co.) is commissioned and built on the Delaware River, near Philadelphia.

1776 – July 4th – Congress declared Independence in Philadelphia.

1776 – December 25th – Washington crosses the Delaware River.[4]

---

[2] "Fort Halifax History." *Fort Halifax Park*. 1 Jan. 2010. Web. 16 May. 2011. <www.forthalifaxpark.org/info.html>.

3

1777 – September 11th – Battle of Brandywine, near Chadds Ford.

1777 – October 4th – Battle of Germantown.

1777 – December 5th – Battle of Whitewash.

1787 – December 12th – Pennsylvania becomes a state.

1790-1800 – Philadelphia was the capital of the United States.

1791-1794 – The Whiskey Rebellion – a tax protest; the "Whiskey Act" became a law in 1791. In 1794, the protests against the act became violent. This issue primarily took place in Western PA.

1800s

1812-1815 – The War of 1812

1822 – Construction begins on Eastern State Penitentiary.

1829 – April 23rd – Eastern State Penitentiary opens. [5]

1861 – 1865 – The American Civil War

1863 – July 1st – July 3rd – Battle of Gettysburg.

1900s

1908 – November 23rd – first patient is admitted to Pennhurst State Hospital.

1971 – mid-1980s – Eastern State Penitentiary is abandoned.

1987 – Pennhurst State School closes.

---

[4] "The Quaker Province: 1681-1776." *Pennsylvania General Assembly*. 1 Jan. 2011. Web. 1 May 2011.
<www.legis.state.pa.us/wu01/vc/visitor_info/pa_history/pa_history.htm>.

[5] "Timeline." *Easter State Penitentiary*. 1 Jan. 2011. Web. 20 May 2011.
<www.easternstate.org/learn/timeline>.

PENNSYLVANIA

"Nowhere in this country, from sea to sea, does nature comfort us with such assurance of plenty, such rich and tranquil beauty as in those unsung unpainted hills of Pennsylvania."

-Rebecca Harding Davis

In the tender, fragile moments during the founding of our nation, a convention took place in Philadelphia, Pennsylvania. Facing the possibility of an inevitable, yet early death, a document was forged, ratified, and the final wording voted upon. It begins with reading of:

> *When in the course of human events, it becomes necessary for one people to dissolve the political bands which have connected them with another, and to assume among the powers of the earth, the separate and equal station to which the Laws of Nature and of Nature's God entitle them, a decent respect to the opinions of mankind requires that they should declare the causes which impel them to separation. We hold these truths to be self-evident, that all men are created equal, that they are endowed by their Creator with certain unalienable Rights, that among these are Life, Liberty and the pursuit of Happiness.[6]*

The document was a Declaration of Independence from England and King George III; it was voted on July 4th, 1776.

All while Congress worked inside a stuffy room; on the battlefields, the

---

[6] "The Declaration of Independence." *Independence Hall Association of Pennsylvania.* 4 July 1995. Web. 20 May. 2011.
<http://www.ushistory.org/declaration/index.htm>.

fiery crack of loaded muskets reverberated through the air. Cannon fire clouded the sky. Across the colonies: American, Native, and British men lay dying from the wounds of war. Their blood soaking the earth, staining the land long after the red is gone.

From the blood soaked land, phantoms have arisen; haunting the state. As the years passed, more unsettled dead have joined their ranks, turning Pennsylvania into one of the most haunted states in the country.

(Old cemetery in Wellsville, PA)

AVONDALE MINE
(LUZERNE COUNTY)

The year was 1869, it was a time where safety precautions were few and child labor was still an allowed concept. There were children in the mines on the disastrous day of September 6th; boys aged twelve through seventeen would account for five of the 110 deaths that day. The remaining number of men were seasoned veterans of the mining industry; used to digging beneath the ground and being aware of any danger that could arise in the cold, dark passages inside of the earth. On the day of September 6th, the men were about to learn that their danger was going to be in the least expected of places, near the surface.

A small fire was built at the bottom of the shaft in order to circulate air through the tunnels. As fires are known to do, it spread, casting itself further into the passage than intended; setting the timbers on fire that framed the mine. Directly above the mine shaft, the breaker collapsed into the mine, completely blocking the only exit to the mine. Slowly the smoke billowed through the mine shaft, choking the air. Though the men above them tried valiantly to save their fellow miners, it was all in vain and the men below ground were left with no hope for a miracle.

One hundred and eight men perished inside the mine. Two others succumbed to poisonous gasses caused by the fire during the rescue effort. No one mining disaster before the year 1900 had claimed as many lives as the Avondale mine disaster. Between the years of 1869 and 1900, no one mining accident was as significant as Avondale either, which is remarkable considering that over 10,000 miners lost their lives on the job between those years. [7]

---

[7] "Avondale Mine Disaster." *Explore PA History.* 1 Jan. 2010. Web. 29 May 2011. <http://explorepahistory.com/hmarker.php?markerid=1-A-ED>.

No matter how technologically advanced our modern world becomes and, despite the safety procedures used to keep miners safe and protected, disaster still happen. When the unfortunate does occur, within minutes rescuers begin their plans to save survivors; radioing and calling for assistance: fire trucks, ambulances, and first responders. To think how different it would have been a hundred years ago without our modern developments.

Paranormal activity at the old abandoned mine is fairly quiet. The spirits of the men still believed to wander the area. Visitors have said that they have heard voices and felt cold spots at the entrance to the mine. None of the miners have come forward to speak their name into a digital recorder to officially tie themselves in with the known history of the mine or the records of those who died there. The ghosts just go about their duties as they did over a century before now. [8]

Directions: Located in Plymouth, Pennsylvania

---

[8] Pike, C. "Avondale Mine Disaster Site, Plymouth, PA." *Phenomenon and Paranormal Investigations: Truth in Evidence*. 1 Jan. 2011. Web. 29 May 2011. <ppiinvestigations.com/avondale.aspx>.

~*~

By definition, a ghost is a deceased person's soul or spirit. It is someone who is dead and gone from out world. Ghosts were once living, breathing humans. In our society, many abhor scientific testing and evaluation and experimentation on other humans, so why should the dead be any different and exempt from societal norms?

The first step in investigating the paranormal should be to remember that they are people with: personalities, stories, history, and emotions. Next is to learn the history: how they may have died, who they were, when did they live? Some of these questions may be answered before or during an investigation. Research is always an important part of paranormal and supernatural investigation. Knowing how a person may have lived or died adds a level of compassion, respect, and intimacy to the investigation at hand.

Knowing that the Avondale miners may have had an agonizing last few moments of life may lead to a more sympathetic interview and study. We do not always have to go to a place expecting to be scared or haunted. Sometimes we can just listen, comfort, and help them to move on.

BELLEMAN'S CHURCH ROAD
(BERKS COUNTY)

Night crept in its casual way, drawing the curtains on the sun. A nippy chill blew through the October air; brushing loose strands of hair across her beautiful face. A shiver ran down her spine, causing her to pull her shawl tighter around her shoulders. The light hearted mood of earlier in the evening grew cold. The party at the neighbor's house had been joyful and then, night came and it was time to go home.

A smile touched rosy lips as her memory reminisced to earlier in the evening, the local young men plying for her affections; older gentlemen remarking on her youthful beauty. Blush leapt to her cheeks at the thought of their compliments. She was not a vain person, truly, nevertheless she could not help but to be flattered by their attentions.

Hearing footsteps fall into place behind her snapped her out of the daydream. The candle lights from earlier dimmed in her memory and were replaced by the night around her. She turned to see the familiar face of one of her suitors silhouetted in the moonlight.

"May I walk you home?" He asked with gentile flare, "A lovely young lady such as yourself should not have to walk alone."

She replied kindly to her admirer, just as any refined farmer's daughter would be expected to respond. He took her arm in his as they walked the long road to her parent's farm. Everywhere around the m was enclosed in night, lighted by only the moon.

As the couple neared the Mohrsville Hotel, her gentlemanly companion stopped suddenly.

"What is it?" she asked.

"Adeline, there is something I must ask you."

"Yes?"

"Will you be my wife?"

She was shocked but, it was not the first time this had happened to her. "I'm sorry, I am not ready to be married yet."

"Is there someone else?"

She looked straight ahead, staring off into the night.

"Your silence gives me my answer," he sneered. Collecting his composure, "you should forget about him. I am the more suitable choice for you out of all those other suitors. Your parents would agree."

"I will see what my father says," she stated as she began to continue her journey home. He grabbed her arms, squeezing, and whipped her around to face him.

"You will marry me, I will see to that."

"No!" Pushing away from him she ran, too frightened to scream. He went after her and grabbed her again, covering her mouth with his hand and dragged her behind the hotel. Kicking and fighting his strangle hold on her, she broke away and tried to run inside for help. This time when he grabbed her, he threw her to the ground.

"I will ask you one last time, will you marry me?"

"Never!" She struggled to her feet, getting tangled in her dress. He pulled her to him as she strained against his pull, trying to get away.

"Look at me!", he commanded, pulling up her chin to look into her face. Adeline shunned away from the jealousy in his eyes disgusted. Enraged he snarled, "you will only belong to me!"

Pulling her father's ax that he had hidden beneath his coat, that he had stolen in case she rejected him; he lifted the axe striking her in the head. Finishing his gruesome killing, he dropped the axe and threw a malicious glance towards the hotel. Seeing no movement inside, he grabbed her lifeless body and headed towards the river. Disappearing into the night.

The body of Adeline Baver was found on October 7th, 1857 near the Mohrsville Hotel by the Dauberville Bridge along the Schuykill Canal. She was nineteen years old. Her body was buried in Salem Belleman's Church cemetery.

News reports from the time were split between reporting that she died of a single axe blow to the head or that her throat was slit by the axe, which came from her father's farm. Police profiled the killer as a jealous admirer, someone who knew Adeline. After the police interrogated all the local young men they found themselves no closer to solving the homicide; and so the killer was free to continue on with life.

Sightings of her ghost have been reported since 1878 along the canal south of Mohrsville toward Dauberville, where she was murdered; and along Belleman's Church Road leading to her gravesite. [9]

Adeline is not the only ghosts along the church road; her spirit is accompanied by that of a man who is believed to be her murderer.

Other ghosts are said to wander the area of Salem Belleman Church, the cemetery, and the road that runs along beside them. Of all these spirits, none are seen as often or are believed to have as tragic of a story of Adeline Baver; the ghosts who wanders waiting for justice to be served to the one who killed her. [10]

---

[9] Adams III, Charles J. "Was Leesport Apparition the Ghost of Adeline Baver?" The Reading Eagle, 3 Mar. 2010. Web. 1 Jan. 2012. <http://www2.readingeagle.com/article.aspx?id=201392>.

[10] "ADALINE BAVER'S GHOST." *Freedom's Corner Haunts & History.* 1 Jan. 2012. Web. 30 Jan. 2012. <https://sites.google.com/site/hauntsandhistory/freedom'scornerhaunts&history>.

- To note: the cemetery where Adeline is buried is an old and historic place. As such, it should be respected by all guests. Those who currently work for this church do not believe the story and state that the area is not haunted at all.

Also, the Black Moon Paranormal Society does not believe in, recommend, or encourage paranormal investigations in cemeteries; unless there are extraordinary accounts of activity or if there is someone in need of help. We believe in letting the dead rest. The ghosts who do wander near Belleman's Church are found beyond the cemetery grounds, on the road named for the church.

Directions: Belleman's Church (Salem Belleman's Church) is located in Mohrsville, Pennsylvania.

BOILING SPRINGS
(CUMBERLAND COUNTY)

Glowing, iridescent in the night, a woman walks the path that runs along Children's Lake. A flowing dream in a white dress, she comes alive in our world. Alone, without a known purpose; no one knows if she is searching for someone or waiting or wandering through our world as she did in life. She is the legendary ghost of the lady of Boiling Springs.

Quaint houses line the road through the town of Boiling Springs. ON one side of the town, the antique Boiling Springs tavern, built around 1832, was once owned by Anheuser-Busch. Within the town, more old houses abound with historic plaques. A few of the most exquisite houses overlook Children's Lake. The lake was meant to be used for the iron industry of old but was eventually transformed into a recreation area. Across from the lake, opposite the direction of the tavern, sits the grist mill. Near the mill lies the remnants of an iron furnace; and within the brush behind the mill is something surprising.

During the day, Boiling Springs seems almost dull and quite; it is a far cry from a bustling city or tourist area. At night, some of the locals say that the area around the lake takes on an energy that cannot be described as anything other than supernatural. This is not astonishing considering that a few parts of the local history were conducted under the cover of night.

In its history, the town was marked as a stop on the Underground Railroad. Daniel Kauffman, who laid out the plans for the village of Boiling Springs, and built his home on Front Street within the town, took control of this "stopover" during the pre-Civil War 1800s. He provided the escaped slaves with food and shelter near his home.

After the flooding in the fall of 2011, a lot of the brush along the Yellow Breeches creek, behind the grist mill, was cleared away to reveal an area of bricks and glass bottles. Considering the trees and the location, it seems as though the shelter for the slaves was uncovered.

While using a digital recorder in the area of the cleared brush, a female spirit can be heard saying the words, "freedom" and "clock." There is a clock tower on the other side of the springs; it was not built until the 1900s in honor of the Veterans of Foreign Wars, wars that occurred in the century after the Civil War, the Emancipation Proclamation that began the freedom of the slaves of the South, and the end of the Underground Railroad.

Also a location for the bustling iron works industry, the Carlisle Iron Works built up around the springs, which had been partially dammed in the 1750s in order to be used by the local industries. It was by the iron furnace stack attached to the industrial works that another ghost was found in the area. [11]

His name is Peter, or at least that is what he told us; a good natured spirit who was willing to answer questions and welcomed visitors. As it is with many ghosts, he is weak from a lack of energy and cannot maintain a conversation for long. The offer was made to him to drain the batteries from the cameras and other equipment to help him communicate with us; nonetheless, he still grew tired and the communication ceased. He only responded one last time with a "yes" in answer to the question, "would you like us to come back and visit you again?"

After walking the path around the lake and asking every question in the paranormal handbook to lure the lady at the lake out, there was not so much as a feminine voice on the digital recorder. Leaving the questions as to who she is still unanswered, if she even exists at all. It is clear that even without the famed lady, there are others in the area who are willing to share their stories.

[11] "Boiling Springs." *Boiling Springs.* 1 Jan. 2012. Web. 10 Mar. 2012. <www.boilingsprings.org>.

CALEDONIA IRON FURANCE
(FRANKLIN CO.)

"…pig iron furnaces so hot a man forgets his fear of hell."
-The Quiet Man (1952) [12]

Thousands of trees line both sides of the road along Pine Grove Road, planted during the Great Depression by the Civilian Conservation Corps to replace the acres cut down for use at the local furnaces. Compared to the well-preserved Pine Grove Iron Furnace located thirteen miles further down the same road; Caledonia Furnace seems to be little more than a rock pile back dropped by a vast forest.

The furnace was originally built in 1837 in the rural area near the Village of Caledonia, located on the Conecocheaque Creek. (Locations for iron furnaces were chosen based primarily on the close proximity of natural resources. This is why so many furnaces are located in the countryside, near forests and water). Caledonia Furnace has been known as Caledonia Works, Caledonia Forge and Steven's Furnace, named for its owner politician Thaddeus Stevens.

In June of 1863, during the American Civil War and the month before the battle at Gettysburg, a Confederate Calvary under the leadership of General Jubal Early burnt the furnace and its surrounding buildings to the ground. This event was an isolated incident by the Confederates in retaliation to Thaddeus Stevens' hate of the South and their way of life.

"I fear we shall forget justice to living rebels and to slaughtered dead, and shall overlook our future safety, and deal too mercifully with assassins

---

[12] *The Quiet Man*. Perf. John Wayne, Maureen O'Hara, Barry Fitzgerald. Republic Pictures, 1952. Film.

and traitors. I can understand how forgiveness should be extended to the ignorant, the poor and deluded; but to permit the ringleaders to escape with impunity, is absolute cruelty. At least, take their property, if you allow them to live. To forgive the penitent is Christian; to suffer the proud murderer to escape, and thus endanger the government, is weakness. Take the riches of those nobles who would found an empire on slavery."

-Thaddeus Stevens

(an excerpt from the speech given by him at Appomattox on April 10, 1865; one day after General Robert E. Lee's surrender to Ulysses S. Grant. In these words, it can be clearly seen his distaste for the Southern Confederacy that he had been outspoken about since the start of the Civil War in 1861.) [13]

Two years after the burning of Caledonia Furnace, the Civil War officially ended. Stevens no longer needed to fear another Confederate attack on his property; yet, from that time until his death on August 11, 1868, Stevens made no effort to rebuild his iron works. The reason assumed to be that the furnace did not generate a good source of income. The land remained untouched until the 1920s, when the Pennsylvania Alpine Club reconstructed the furnace and the blacksmith shop. The reconstructed stack is only about half the size, possibly less, of the original furnace and it's questionable if it stands in the same location as the original. [14]

Throughout this book, there are several sections on iron furnaces, which may seem surprising since iron furnace are not tied to hundreds or thousands of deaths such as one would find on a battlefield or in a hospital. In spite of this, furnaces have been able to draw in the paranormal. I will spend the next few paragraphs delving into the reasons why this happens.

Iron furnaces were incredibly dangerous places to work and fatal accidents did happen; though it is rare to find a historical recording of many

---

[13] Stevens, Thaddeus. "Speech of Mr. Stevens at the Public Meeting in the Court House on Monday, April 10." *Thaddeus Stevens Papers On-line*. Transcribed Cordes Ford. Proof. Brad Burgess. Furman University, 10 Apr. 1865. Web. 10 Apr. 2011. <http://history.furman.edu/benson/hst41/red/stevens3.htm>.

[14] Washlaski, Raymond A., and Ryan A. Washlaski. "Caledonia Furnace Caledonia Forge." *Pa Iron Works*. Rootsweb.ancestry, 1 Jan. 2002. Web. 19 Apr. 2011. <http://paironworks.rootsweb.ancestry.com/fracaledonia.html>.

people dying while working there. In the case of Caledonia, there are no documented incidents. This does not mean that nothing significant happened, just possibly though, some things were not recorded.

Workers could suffer from heat stroke, eye disease, asthma, and other health problems related to being exposed to toxic fumes. There was the chance of explosions, if moisture was able to get close to the melting ore. Plus, the dangers associated with cutting down trees for charcoal production and mining. Any loss of life or a grievous injury would not have been completely unexpected; although most workers would have felt their wounds in their later years. In a time of limited medical knowledge and care, paired with no health insurance, even minor injuries could have drastic consequences. Many furnaces operated on the edge of bankruptcy causing both owners and employees to do without many aspects of care.

Around sixty workers would be employed at the furnace. A dozen men well-versed in the iron work would be at the stack: melting the ore, feeding the fire, and running the operations. The rest would be chopping down trees, mining the quarries, and making charcoal. Charcoal production could use up to an acre of forest a day. [15]

The question does remain, if an iron furnace did not have any significant causalities, if any at all, how is it that paranormal phenomena are documented to occur around so many of them? This answer may lay in the category of residual haunting. In this classification of haunting, the ghost does not interact with the living world. They are on a loop in the past, a replaying video, and they just simply are there stuck in time. These men do not know that you exist and they do not know that they are dead. (To note: there are insistences that have been sited where a residual haunting occurs and the person is not dead. While this is viewed by many cultures as a bad omen; it shows a power to energy and time that we do not fully understand yet.)

Time can be affected by vast amounts of energy: emotional, physical, or mental energy; causing time loops to occur and leaving a residual energy. This is one of several theories out there on how and why residual hauntings do occur (this is the one to which I subscribe my own beliefs.) When a man worked at an iron furnace, his entire life revolved around it. Small

---

[15] "Description and Operation." *Iron Furnaces*. Old Industry, 1 Jan. 2011. Web. 15 March 2011.
<www.oldindustry.org/OH_HTML/OH_Buckeye.html#Description>

communities would build themselves around the location. The workers were always nearby and on constant alert to make sure that the fire would not spread to the nearby forest.

Little is known about the working conditions however; at other similar iron furnaces, there is documentation of twelve hour shifts with an operation time of twenty-four hours a day, nine months out of the year. With the other three months being used to clean and perform maintenance on the stack. With so much of their life's energy being spent committed to their job, it would not surprising if some of that energy was left behind.

Another theory, depending on how you would view it, is that residual energies are trapped into rocks in the earth. Certain stones: quartz, limestone, and magnetite; specifically, are the ones that hold this energy. There is, I must stress, no real scientific proof of such stones causing residual energy, if there were then the work of paranormal researchers and investigators would be further along. As it is with the paranormal, this is merely a stated idea to explain what is yet unexplainable.

Now that all the background information for this furnace has been completed, on to who and what was found by the paranormal investigators at Caledonia Furnace. With historical facts backing that male workers and soldiers would have been at the furnace, it is quite remarkable that the EVP that was caught was of a female spirit.

April 19th, 2011 at 5:48 p.m.

Investigator: *"What is your name?"*
"It's Jennifer." Her answer was loud but soft, clear, and without an accent.

Since there is so little information on this particular furnace, it is impossible to tell why Jennifer would be in this location. The owner, Thaddeus Stevens, was not married and had no children. Not only that, but he did not live in the area. This concludes that the ghost has no ties to him. She could be the wife of a worker, perhaps, or someone linked to another era before or after the furnace was built and in operation. For now, Jennifer remains our mysterious ghosts, which leads to more questions than answers…so far.

"I should fear to be haunted by the ghosts of murdered patriots stalking forth from their premature grave in their blood shrouds."

-Thaddeus Stevens (Appomattox, April 10th, 1865)

Directions: The furnace is located at the intersection of Route 30 and Pine Grove Furnace Road, near Chambersburg and Gettysburg.

CHICKIES ROCK
(LANCASTER COUNTY)

Rhythmic and powerful, the steady drumming from Native American hide drums echoes across the Susquehanna River and up the steep treacherous cliff called Chickies Rock charging the adrenaline of those living to the beat of the drum and striking fear into their enemies; all except for the dark shadows hiding in the woods around them, quietly listening, watching, and waiting.

In elementary school there was this game we used to play where our teacher would line us up in the hallway, or classroom, and tell the first person in line a sentence. Whatever the teacher said would then be passed person to person down the way. The guarantee was that the story would change between the first and the last person. I believe this was called the telephone game, and the so-called moral was to teach us how rumors and stories can change so as to not always believe what you hear about someone.

Oral traditions are of the same mold; which is how the most popular legend of Chickies Rock, and I would dare say one of the most famous stories in Lancaster County, has come to have three different versions. All three tales start the same; a young man and a young woman from the Susquehannock tribe nation fell in love. They used the top of the rocky cliffs as their rendezvous point. In one tale, the couple's love was forbidden and they could not marry because of tribal costumes. Instead of facing their mortal lives apart from each other, they made a suicide pact and jumped from the top of the cliff.

The second version is slightly different with the young man dying in battle; and the woman, in her grief stricken state, leapt alone off the cliff. In the third, and most romanticized and retold version, it once again begins speaking of the love between the couple. Although this time, neither death nor forbidden love stands between them; it is her heart's betrayal for another.

One night, the young Susquehannock maiden met her old lover to break the news that she was in love with someone else. Not just anyone had caught her eye but it was one of the white settlers who had come to the area. In a jealous act for vengeance, her scorned lover lunged at her. All the while, waiting nearby, the settler hears her screams and runs to save her, only to find that he is no match for her former lover. The settler's throat is slit and he is left to die. His conquering attacker gathers the terrified woman into his arms and leaps off of the cliff. It is said that the ghost of the settler, beaten and bloodied, still wanders the woods searching for his lost love.

This tale is oddly similar to another legend that took place roughly a hundred miles (or a two hour drive) from Chickies Rock at Penn's Cave; an exquisite natural masterpiece that is filled with a lake. In this tale, a young Native American woman fell in love with a white settler; her name was Nittanie, from whom the Penn State Nittany lion mascot is said to have acquired its name. The man involved in this story had been give the name of Malachi Boyer. Knowing that their love was forbidden, they decided upon the path of fleeing in the hope of a new life together. Sadly, fate would decree a different culmination, the two lovers were captured and Malachi was taken to Penn's Cave and thrown in the water to drown. All the while he was calling out the name of his lost love. [16]

The local legends of Chickies Rock do not end with the Native Americans. At some point in the years following the deaths of the ill-fate couple; another tale arose about an old woman who lived on the land near the rocks. She was forced from her home, possibly so that the few iron furnaces at the location could be built. In retaliation she cursed the earth. Little else I known of the woman, there are no records to indicate that she even existed. Whether or not one wants to believe that someone cursed the land, the future tragedies in the years to come are quite an ill-fated coincidence. [17]

Between the time of the local legends from the 1700s and earlier, to the Civil War and Industrial Revolution in the 1800s; little is recorded as

[16] "History." *Penn's Cave and Wildlife Park*. 1 Jan. 2011. Web. 12 Apr. 2011. <www.pennscave.com/history.php>.

[17] Gulley, Rosemary Ellen. "Chickies Rock." *Ghost Hunting Pennsylvania*. Birmingham: Clerisy, 2009. 129. Print.

happening in the area. If any accidents, suicides, or murders occurred, they have long since been lost to time and those involved lingering and cold in their graves. Only rumors dictate that there is more to the location's history than what is known to us and written now.

From the late 1800s through the early 1900s, as the Industrial Revolution swept the country; a railroad, canal, and trolley line were built in Chickies Park and an amusement park was set up. This peaceful, recreation era was to be short lived, ending in 1896 when one of the trolley cars crashed on its way to the nearby town of Columbia, killing six people and injuring many others.

March 6th, 2010
- Walking the trail towards the top of the cliff.
- Times are written as hour-minute-seconds.

3:20:57 p.m. – Investigator – "I don't know where the trolley was."

3:21:00 p.m. – Digital Recorder Response – "I will show you." – male voice.

3:21:02 p.m. – DRR – "God." – male voice, different from above.

3:21:24 p.m. – Investigator – "Should we walk around and down?"

3:21:26 p.m. – DRR – "Down the side." – female voice.

November 27th, 2010
- Walking the trail towards the top of the cliff.

1:35:23 p.m. – DRR – "Why are you here?" – male voice.

1:37:05 p.m. – DRR – banging noise.

1:37:28 p.m. – DRR – "Help us!" – male voice.

1:38:35 p.m. – DRR – Cough

1:41:31 p.m. – DRR – Woman's laughter.

1:43:37 p.m. – DRR – Noise that sounds like metal banging on metal.

1:53:20 p.m. – Investigator – "I thought that the trolley live was up further."

1:53:28 p.m. – DRR – "No!" – male voice.

- Going off the path and into the woods.

1:54:12 p.m. – DRR – "Come back!" – male voice.

1:57:54 p.m. – DRR – "Hey Bert, here they come" – male voice.

2:02:11 p.m. – DRR – Noise of bang, bang, bang.

2:06:02 p.m. – DRR – Inaudible

2:07:23 p.m. – DRR – Male voice saying what sounds like, "peekaboo."

2:08:02 p.m. – DRR – "Wow!" – male voice.

2:09:12 p.m. – DRR – Rattling sound.

Witnesses say that some of the canal workers also haunt the area; remaining in a residual form and unable to further communicate or ask questions. A man killed in a river boat accident is also said to haunt the area. [18]

By the 1930s, most of the attractions, with the exception of the railroad which was still in use, were abandoned. Unfortunately, similar to other locations with high up, breath taking views, Chickies Rock has dealt with numerous suicides over the years, a number that continues to grow every few years. Although not every person who has fallen from the rocks are believed to have done so on purpose; a few show off and drunken people have stepped carelessly on the overhanging rocks. Despite the fact that there is a fence there with warning signs ordering people not to cross over the edge. The spirits of these poor souls are also aid to still wander sad and terrified to the cliff's edge, crying, and praying.

March 6th, 2010

- At the fence at the top of the cliff

3:28:07 p.m. – Investigator – "What is your name?"
3:28:08 p.m. – DRR – "William" – male voice.

How many people have died, no one knows for certain except for perhaps the mysterious shadow people that are said to have inhabited the area since the time of the Native American tribes. These shadowy beings of non-human origin are a mysterious supernatural phenomenon in the world of the paranormal. The shadow people of Chickies Rock do little other than

---

[18] Nesbitt, Mark, and Patty A. Wilson. "The Ghostly Screams of Chickies Rock." *The Big Book of Pennsylvania Ghost Stories*. Stackpole, 2008. 116-119. Print.

exist and watch the world pass. Beliefs about these creatures have ranged from them being benevolent, too subdued, too malicious.

In 1863, during the American Civil War, a Union post was briefly set up at the area called the Breezyview Overlook, (which is to the left of the cliff that we were talking about at the beginning of this chapter.) The point of the post was to keep an eye on the Confederate forces in Wrightsville, across the river.

My first investigation ever at Chickies Rock Park began at the Overlook; patches of unmelted snow littered the grassy area around the gazebo. The terrible cold was worth the pain to see the breathtaking view at this location. The activity started immediately after I stepped out of the car and turned on the digital recorder. First there were two loud bands, which were not from any car doors slamming shut. Then for several seconds, a woman can be heard sobbing as we made our way across the grass, past the gazebo to the fence that stops people from walking off of the edge. Following the fence to the left, it took us to an area filled with trees. Two more EVPs came over the recorder at this time, a woman's scream and a man's husky mumbled "wait." Perhaps it is because of events like the woman's terrified high pitch scream are why some psychic visitors to the area believe that a few murders have gone unrecorded in the vicinity. The investigations that took place after this initial viewing were even more eventful.

November 27th, 2010

2:24:00 p.m. – Investigator – "What is your name?"

2:24:08 p.m. – Digital Recorder Response – "Karen" – female voice.

2:24:25 p.m. – Investigator – "Why are you here?"

2:24:33 p.m. – Investigator – "I would guess most of this is residual."

2:24:41 p.m. – DRR – "Yes" or "Guess" – male voice.

2:27:55 p.m. – DRR – "Adam" (One of the investigators is named Adam)

2:27:57 p.m. – DRR – Male voice says something that sounds like "Obershaw."

From the top of the Breezyview Overlook, if the reader takes a right, there is a path that leads down the steep cliff to the bottom near the railroad tracks. The path is called the Susquehanna Trail.

- Walking on the Susquehanna Trail

2:34:44 p.m. – DRR – "Ok" – female voice.

2:35:54 p.m. – DRR – "Hum" – female voice.

2:36:55 p.m. – Personal Experience – Investigator hears a voice but cannot make out the words.
2:47:44 p.m. – Personal Experience – Investigator heard a loud rattling sound.
2:48:04 p.m. – DRR – "Hello" – male voice.

2:48:12 p.m. – DRR – "Hello" – male voice that sounds different from the first "hello."

- At the bottom of the stairs.

2:58:28 p.m. – Personal Experience – Investigator hears a drumming sound

that is vibrating the air. (Which goes along with the claims of people hearing Native American drums at the base of the cliff.)
2:59:19 p.m. – Personal Experience – Two investigators hear the drumming sound.

November 27th, 2010

- Near the Susquehanna Trail
2:44:27 p.m. – Personal Experience – Investigator hears loud undistinguishable noise, heard on the digital recorder too.
2:44:58 p.m. – DRR – "I will make them pay for this."

I believe that the voice that was captured on the recording saying, "I will make them pay for this," may very well be the ghost that others have reported being in the tunnel on the Susquehanna Trail. Although the local story is that he died after being hit by a train; but by the wording of that sentence, it seems as if it may have been more than a mere accident. For now, the answer to that still remains unclear.

Directions: On PA – 441 between Marietta and Columbia, PA.

- **Note:** Chickies Rock is not for the faint of heart, or for those who are empathic when it comes to spirits. Chickies is a place that holds a dark energy in some places, most likely because of the numerous tragedies that have occurred in that area. There have been instances of people playing around on the cliff and falling. Also, keep in mind that it is illegal to cross over the fence there. During certain parts of the year, hunters are in the area.

CODORUS IRON FURNACE
(YORK COUNTY)

The sun shines high above the old, abandoned Codorus Iron Furance works. Behind the stone stack, a forest of trees reaches towards the sunny sky; spreading their green leaves wide. Within the rows of brown tree trunks and green foliage, a figure in white appears; the layers of her dress blowing in the wind, casting a clichéd ghastly image. Her face and hair shielded by a white veil; silently she walks through the trees, down the hill towards the furnace stack. The living calls out to her with no reply. Hauntingly, sadly she wanders our world alone, helping the occasional lost travelers on the twisting backwoods roads of York County by walking in the direction that they want to go. Perhaps she is waiting for someone to help her find her own way home.

Countless stories from all across the nation recount the tale of a female apparition that addresses her by the color of the gown she is wearing. Ladies in: white, green, blue, red, and black are all common lace stories within every state. As for this particular lady, no one knows who she is, was, or why she still walks through the trees near the furnace. It is speculated that she was either a wife or mistress to one of the furnace masters and that he likely killed her for any number of various reasons. Perhaps she was a pregnant mistress or an unwanted wife? Or just a woman with no ties to the furnace at all, there are several haunted locations on that side of York County and she could be tied to anyone. If you are fortunate enough to find her and hear her speak, maybe you will be the lucky one to find the answers.

November 20th, 2010

2:18 p.m. – Personal Experience – Investigator hears what sounds like a disembodied female scream.

Amidst the tress, near the acclaimed haunted Accomac Inn, and next to the Codorus Creek rests what is left of the Codorus Iron works. All that remains of the iron community is the stone stack of the furnace. Tax records from 1798 say that one log home, plus workmen's houses, a barn, mill, and several other buildings were listed on the property of the furnace; none of the remnants of which exists today.

The furnace was built in 1765 by William Bennet. By the records and rumors of history, the furnace was not very profitable and it was forced to cease operations in 1850. Many iron furnaces operated on the verge of closing and bankruptcy; so for one to fail was not a surprise. The one boost to the poor furnace community was that it supplied ammunitions to the Continental Army stationed at Valley Forge during the winter of 1777. [19]

November 20th, 2010

2:20:55 p.m. - Investigator - "Are there any soldiers here that were killed by cannon balls manufactured here?"

2:21:29 p.m. - Digital Recorder Response - "Yes!" - male voice.

It has been theorized that some spirits haunt the areas that caused their pain and death. If one believes the hauntings, the Remington Arms Factory is an example of this type of phenomenon. While the soldier may have died on a battlefield somewhere else; the instrument that caused his death came from somewhere else. That is why we may find a few bitter souls in the most unexpected places for them to be heard.

November 20th, 2010

2:16:53 p.m. – DRR – "Hi" – male voice.
2:17:10 p.m. – DRR – "Don't touch the girl." – male voice.
2:20:55 p.m. – Personal Experience – Investigator feels something resembling a spider web touching her; but there was no web.

December 4th, 2010

---

[19] "Codorus Furnace." *Hellam Township.* 1 Jan. 2011. Web. 31 Mar. 2011. <http://www.hellamtownship.com/index.asp?Type=B_BASIC&SEC=%7B1432E 3D0-BDBF-45F8-9543-4CA759619B4C%7D>.

1:01:59 p.m. – Investigator – "What is your name?"

1:02:02 p.m. – DRR – "Peter" – male voice.

1:02:20 p.m. – Personal Experience – Investigator hears a child's voice.

1:03:27 p.m. – Personal Experience – Investigator asks if anyone was there and heard an audible "yes," not caught on the recording.

1:03:33 p.m. – EMF – Spike high

1:06:27 p.m. – Personal Experience – Investigator hears a dripping sound.

1:07:44 p.m. – Personal Experience – Investigator hears a "psst."

1:08:35 p.m. – Personal Experience – Investigator hears a knocking and a dripping sound.

1:10:22 p.m. – DRR – "Hi" – male voice.

1:25:12 p.m. – Personal Experience – Investigator hears a horse and cart being pulled.

Directions: Located near the Accomac Inn off of Accomac Road in Hellam Township, York County.

COLEBROOK/CORNWALL FURNACE
(LANCASTER/LEBANON COUNTY)

Can animals be ghosts or spirits of an intelligent nature? That is a long standing topic of discussion in the paranormal world. Most would say, "no!" Though, there are people who have had pets pass on to the other side that claim to still feel the presence of that animal. Seeing a shadow run across the floor out of the corner of their eyes; feeling movement on a bed as though the pet was climbing into bed to sleep with them, just as it always did. All of these accounts could easily be passed off as residual. That does not mean that they always are, there are accounts of pets coming back only in a time of despair to comfort or; in at least one instance, to remind the owner of the sins in his own life.

The October night was cold, most of the men in the hunting party would have rather been back inside continuing to drink near a warm fireplace. Unfortunately for them, their host had other ideas. Peter Grubb was a boastful man, he was a man who loved to hunt and drink. This particular night's claim was that he had the greatest hunting hounds in the area. After drinking well beyond a reasonable level, he took his guests out into the chilly night to show the impressiveness of his dogs.

After a long round of hunting, the dogs did not bring home the game. It was the first time they had ever failed to not prove their worthiness to their master. In a fit of his infamous temper, Grubb ordered the entire pack thrown into the furnace fires. The hunting party, servants, and the dog's handler pleaded with him not to do it. After threating the men with physical violence and their jobs, the dogs were thrown into the fire; including Flora, the pack leader and the one dog that seemed to have had a bond with her master (the rumors say one night she saved his life when he collapsed drunk

33

in the snow).

In the days following the terrible deed, not surprisingly Grubb's social circle shrank quickly. He lost the few that he could consider "friends." They say he went mad, muttering to himself and being chased by a ghostly pack of hounds led by Flora. Ironically, the legend says that he died out in the snow after being chased by the invisible hounds; just as he would have a night years before if Flora would not have saved his life. [20]

Years of this account range in the 1790s to 1800. The storied of the ghostly pack began immediately after the event and; it is said that the ghostly pack can be heard chasing after prey as they did on their last, fateful hunt. Howling into the wind and traveling through the area around the furnace. Every October, the reenactment occurs again and again and again.

There is some confusion as to whether the hounds inhabit Cornwall or Colebrook furnace. Both were owned by the Grubb family, which was common with iron furnaces in Pennsylvania. One family would own and operate several furnaces and then different people would manage them. Cornwall furnace does still exist in Cornwall, Lebanon County, and it is a historic landmark complete with tours through the site. The furnace was built in 1742. Colebrook furnace was built in 1791, along the Conewago Creek in Colebrook, Lancaster County. The Colebrook was dismantled in 1858.

Directions to Cornwall Furnace: 94 Rexmont Road, Cornwall

---

[20] Asfar, Dan. "The Hounds of Colebrook Furnace." *Ghost Stories of Pennsylvania.* Lone Pine International, 2002. 172-182. Print.

FORT HUNTER
(DAUPHIN COUNTY)

People, animals, land they all have a life energy attached to them. It is an energy that can feed off of and can influence one another in subtle ways. This energy can be transferred to non-living objects: precious things like a favorite doll, an engagement ring, or a wedding gown. Or it can be given to objects of destruction: a sword, a knife, or a gun. These objects can carry with them their owner's energy, causing a haunting to happen where there was no one until the object was introduced to the environment; inside of Fort Hunter mansion are hundreds of remnants and antiques of the past; each with an equal chance of having an aura of energy.

Years before Fort Hunter took on the beautiful scenic appearance of how it looks today; the land was used as a mill and a fort during the trying time around and during the French and Indian War. With its useful location along the Susquehanna River, it was one of several locations used by the British to build a garrison and communication center. The fort no longer exists and archaeological digs were recently commenced on the property to find where the tiny fort actually stood. Although common sense would say that the fort would have been close to where the present day mansion sits with its panoramic view of the river; giving the watchers at the fort a perfect view to spot any approaching enemy. During a tour that was taken during a field trip to the location years ago, our guide suggested the same thing.

The fort was used and abandoned twice during its sort life. Building the forts along the Susquehanna River began in 1756; this particular fort is rarely mentioned after July 1758. Which means it was probably abandoned about this time as the battles during the French and India War shifted elsewhere. Directly after the end of the war, a new Native American threat began under the leadership of Chief Pontiac and has since been known as Pontiac's Rebellion. In fear of their families and property, the local settlers used Fort Hunter as a meeting point before they traveled to Fort Augusta. Once this rebellion was crushed, the fort was deserted again.

Fort Hunter was named for Samuel Hunter, who married Catherine Chambers, the widow of the original owner, Joseph Chambers. Chambers was of the same family as the founder of Chambersburg, Pennsylvania. After the fall of Pontiac's Rebellion, Hunter officially purchased the land and within days, had sold the property to its next owners, John and Mary Garber. The Garber family is rarely mentioned in the history of the fort and seems to have done little with the property, even though they lived there for seventeen years. It is believed that they built a house on the property; which was replaced with the mansion. Their names have become overshadowed by the man and family who came after them, the family for whom the beautiful mansion was built.

Archibald McAllister was a veteran of the American Revolution and a prominent citizen of the Harrisburg area. He took a great deal of time and love in the property at Fort Hunter; building the mansion, springhouse, barn, ice house, and diary that still stand today. For eighty-three years, the property remained in possession of the family, passing from father to his son, John Carson; and from John to his children.

One has to think though, is McAllister built the current residence on the property; what did the property and house look like before that time. What hidden secrets and stories are missing from the history? Just like the original fort, they have become nothing more than experiences in the past.

John Carson McAllister passed away in 1866, leaving the property to be divided by his heirs. Instead of keeping their families once beloved home, the family sold the property and all its buildings to Daniel Dick Boas and his wife Margaret Bates Boas. Eventually, their youngest daughter Helen and her husband John W. Reily would become the last family to live in the mansion; where they would live until their deaths, with John passing in 1927 and Helen in 1932.

Daniel Dick Boas is the only recorded family member of any of the families that owned the property to have died tragically. He had been coming home one night from the country, when he was injured in a carriage accident. County Commissioner S. Boyd Martin was with him at the time of the accident but; it is not known who was driving the carriage. Boas was taken back to his mansion where he died soon afterwards. [21]

---

[21] Dickson, Carl A. *Fort Hunter Mansion and Park: A Guide*. Mechanicsburg: Stackpole, 2002. 7-32. Print.

If you happen to drive down Front Street in Harrisburg; many of the names in this chapter may seem familiar to you. Considering that some of these names are now street names in the city. Just to give an example of how prominent these families were to the city of Harrisburg.

With only one supposed death in the home, and with a rather uneventful history, it does not seem like Fort Hunter has what it usually takes to be a haunted location. However, tragedy and bloodshed are not always needed to make a location active. Sometimes the fulfillment of life in happy times, in a happy home, is all that is needed. Why would someone want to leave the home that they knew and loved in life for the unknown of the hereafter?

Visitors to the fort seem to be drawn to three different spots on the property: the mansion, the river, and the gardens in the back right corner by the mansion. Perhaps a previous inhabitant of the house is guiding the way?

February 20th, 2010

* By the river, beside the mansion.

1:31:15 p.m. – DRR – "Water" – male voice.

* Walking past the front porch of the mansion.

1:37:10 p.m. – DRR – "Come in!" – female voice.

March 7th, 2010

4:13:15 p.m. – DRR – "We have guests." – male voice.
4:14:36 p.m. – Investigator – "Let's walk over to the river."
4:15:02 p.m. – DRR – "Okay!" – male voice.

*Walking past the front of the mansion

4:17:03 p.m. – DRR – "Wait!" – male voice.
4:17:11 p.m. – DRR – "Come closer!" – male voice.
4:17:54 p.m. – DRR – "Hello" – breathy female whisper.

March 25th, 2010

*By the gardens

3:01:02 p.m. – DRR – "F***!" – male voice.
3:01:04 p.m. – DRR – "I just killed _____." – male voice.

March 27th, 2010

*By the front porch of the mansion.

10:03:47 a.m. – Investigator – Hears a knocking sound on the front porch of the mansion.
10:13:53 a.m. – DRR – "I just need your kiss." – female voice.

*By the covered bridge on the property.

10:29:41 a.m. – DRR – Whispering.
10:29:42 a.m. – Temperature Change.
10:33:22 a.m. – DRR – Laughter.

While walking through the bridge during our investigation, the EMF d3etector did blink caution several times in different areas of the bridge. However, this was debunked because of power lines being close by.

April 29th, 2011

*Back side of the mansion.

12:40:22 p.m. – Investigator – "Is there anybody here?"
12:40:28 p.m. – DRR – "Just me" – young female voice.

FORT MIFFLIN
(PHILADELPHIA COUNTY)

William H. Howe was not what one would necessarily call a perfect soldier. Perhaps in death he is haunted by the final choices he made in his life; the very same choices that led him to the gallows at Fort Mifflin on May 26th, 1864. It is believed that his ghost still roams the grounds, especially the cell he stayed in while waiting on a pardon that never came. The story behind the ghost of Howe happened in the later years of the fort; so let us go back to the beginning.

Located on Mud Island on the Delaware River near Philadelphia, Fort Mifflin was commissioned by the British in 1771. Ironically, it would end up helping the Americans forces during the American Revolution a few years later. Over the course of five weeks in 1777, 400 Continental soldiers held off a barrage of cannon balls by the British Navy. In total, 10,000 cannon balls were fired on the fort, costing the Americans over 150 soldiers. Eventually the Americans evacuated the fort, but not before General George Washington and the rest of the army were encamped at Valley Forge for the winter. It would not be until the spring of 1778 that the armies would meet again.

During the 1790s, the fort was rebuilt to repair the damage done during the Revolution; in time for the War of 1812, when the Americans would again face the British Army. In the 1860s, Fort Mifflin was used as a prisoner of war camp for the Civil War. While the main purpose was for housing Confederates, a few exceptions were made for traitors and deserters of the Union Army. The latter reason is how William Howe found his way to a small cell within the fort's compound.

Howe had joined the Union Army in time for the disastrous Union defeat at the Battle of Fredericksburg in Virginia. Various genealogical and ancestry sites list his date of birth as being around 1839, making him approximately twenty-three-years-old at the time of the battle.[22] By all reports, he fought bravely during the battle; at the conclusion of which, 1,284 of his fellow soldiers were dead, with another 9,600 wounded, and 1,769 captured or missing. Howe was listed among the wounded, and between the wounds and a serious illness that the caught, he left the army and went home to his wife.

When, inevitably, other Union soldiers arrived at his home to arrest him for desertion, he tried to escape. During this failed attempt, he murdered one of the soldiers; adding to the charges against him. Two years and five months after the battle of Fredericksburg, Howe was hanged.

After the Civil War, the fort saw very little action. During World War I and World War II, it was used as an ammunitions depot. The fort was owned by the United States Army until 1952, when it was turned over to the city of Philadelphia. [23]

Besides Howe, it is said that a screaming woman also haunts the fort. Differing reports dispute the name, however, most call her Elizabeth. Whoever she is, more than one person has recounted to me of hearing her chilling scream from inside the fort. The ghost of Jacob the blacksmith also haunts the fort in the area of the Blacksmith's shop; making a racket as he toils away.

Twelve buildings still stand on the fort grounds: the Arsenal, Artillery Shed, Soldier's Barracks, Officer's Quarters, Commandant's House, West Sally port, the Hospital, Casemates, East Magazine, and Casemate 11. Casemates are enclosures used to shelter soldiers during attacks and prisoners during the Civil War. Of these buildings: the Officer's Quarters, the Blacksmith Shop, and Casemate 11 are reportedly the most haunted.

Casemate 11 was discovered quite by accident in 2006. A caretaker was mowing the grass when his leg fell through a hole. After digging up the area, the cell was discovered; and inside, carved into the stone wall, read the

---

[22] "William. Howe of Mont. Co. Pa, Executed Fort Mifflin 1864; Info and Descendants." *Howe Family Genealogy Forum*. 10 March. 2008. Web. 20 May 2011. <http://genforum.genealogy.com/howe/messages/4597.html>.

[23] "Fort Mifflin." *Fort MIfflin: The Fort That Saved America*. 1 Jan. 2011. Web. 15 May 2011. <http://fortmifflin.us//about.html>.

name 'William H. Howe'. [24]

Directions: Fort Mifflin and Hog Island Roads, Philadelphia

---

[24] "Historic Discovery Made at Fort Mifflin." *11th Pennsylvania Regiment.* 1 Jan. 2006. Web. 1 Jan. 2011. <http://www.11thpa.org/mifflin_find.html>.

FORT NECESSITY
AND
THE BATTLE OF THE MONONGAHELA
(BRADDOCK'S DEFEAT) AND MOUNT
WASHINGTON TAVERN
(ALLEGHENY COUNTY AND FAYETTE COUNTY)

Some places offer only the slightest glimpse into the paranormal. A singular occurrence or story with a little history tied in. Hardly worth the trip for most people; but when combined with other similar and connected places, the effect is much more dramatic.

Fort Necessity is one of the beginning marks of the French and Indian War and the sight of the only time George Washington, one of our greatest generals (not to mention our first President), surrendered to enemy forces. Conflicts between the British and the French, along with their colonists and Native American allies, had been escalating for some time. Both the British and the French had begun to construct forts in the area of the Ohio River. One of the British fortifications, called Fort LeBeouf, had been taken over by the French and was reconstructed as Fort Duquesne. [25]

Forces under George Washington had been sent by the governor of Virginia, Governor Dinwiddie, into French territory in the region to order them to leave. Washington was given additional orders to collect as many men and supplies on his way as he could. As Washington and his group of soldiers, Native Americans (Mingo warriors under the command of Tanacharison) and colonists, reached near what is now Uniontown; they ambushed the French encampment commanded by Joseph Coulon de

---

[25] "The French and Indian War in Pennsylvania." *Explore PA History.* 1 Jan. 2010. Web. 29 May 2011.
<http://explorepahistory.com/hmarker.php?markerid=1-A-ED>.

Villiers de Jumonville. Jumonville had been sent ahead to warn Washington against coming into French territory. This ambush on May 28, 1754, came to be known as the Battle of Jumonville Glen; and was the beginning of the French and Indian War. The attack lasted fifteen minutes, and during it, Jumonville was killed.

Aware that a counter-attack was imminent, Washington repositioned his men at "Great Meadows," west of the Allegheny Mountains. On June 3, his men had completed construction of the effort that was aptly named Fort Necessity. The structure was little more than a hut for ammunition and a circular stockade; nevertheless, it had to do for on July 3, at 11am, the French attacked the fort.

Jumonville's older brother, Louis Coulon de Villiers, led the attack. De Villiers attacked the fort once, and then due to a miscalculation as to the location of Necessity, he ordered his men to regroup in the woods. This gave Washington's men enough time to regroup. A number of things then happened to bring about the downfall of the British troops. One being that, during the battle, the Virginians retreated back into the fort; leaving Washington and the British outnumbered by the French. This, in turn, led to the British also having to return to the fort. Then it began to rain so heavily, the gunpowder became wet and could no longer be used. [26]

The saving grace for Washington's men was that de Villiers feared British reinforcements could arrive at any moment. With the mounting difficulties on both sides, negotiations were worked out and Washington surrendered the fort. Afterward, the Virginians returned to their colony. [27]

Within the woods where the French had to regroup during the battle, full-body apparitions of these soldiers have been seen, though they quickly fade away as they march further into the trees. Near where the reconstructed stockade was built, there is a visitor's center that provides information about the battle; in the center at night, and footsteps can be heard walking the floors. Visitors have also reported hearing the sounds of

---

[26] "The Battle of Fort Necessity." *National Park Service*. Web. 6 June 2011. <www.nps.gov/fone/battle.htm>.

phantom muskets firing and then fading into the wind. [28]

Mount Washington Tavern

Near the location of Fort Necessity, within the compounds of the park, there is the Mount Washington Tavern. In 1770, George Washington purchased the land that was the sight of the battle; and in the 1830s, Judge Nathanial Ewing of Uniontown, built the tavern. James Sampey bought the tavern in 1840; he ran it until 1855. The reason the Sampey family sold the property was because railroads were being built up and growing in popularity. With railroads, there was less profit in running a roadside tavern.

The Fazenbaker family was the last owners of the place and using the location as a private residence until the state took it over in 1932. Now that you have all the family names associated with the property; keep in mind that such information is beneficial when asking questions about the apparitions inside the location.

As for the apparition who has appeared in this one, the description is as follows:

His clothing is reminiscent of a bartender in an old Hollywood movie, with balding, dark hair and a small dark moustache. He was a large, heavy set man. His white shirt and apron did little to hid his girth. Speculatively, he eyed the woman watching him. Within seconds of the woman seeing him, he disappeared into the air. He has yet to be seen again. [29]

Braddock's Defeat

"The officers behaved gallantly, in order to encourage their men, for which they suffered greatly, there being near sixty killed and wounded; a large proportion of the number we had.
The Virginian troops showed a good deal of bravery, and were nearly all killed; for I believe, out of three companies that were there, scarcely thirty men are left

---

[28] "Fort Necessity: Farmington, Pennsylvania." *Grave Addiction.* 1 Jan. 2011. Web. 1 Jan. 2011. <www.graveaddiction.com/mtwashtav.html7/16/12>.

[29] "Mount Washington Tavern, Farmington, Pennsylvania." *Grave Addiction.* 1 Jan. 2011. Web. 1 Jan. 2011. <www.graveaddiction.com/mtwashtav.html7/16/12>.

alive. Captain Peyrouny, and all his officers down to a corporal were killed, Captain Polson had nearly as hard a fate, for only one of his was left. In short, the dastardly behavior of those they call regulars exposed all others, that were inclined to do their duty, to almost certain death; and, at last, in despite of all the efforts of the officers to the contrary, they ran, as sheep pursued by dogs, and it was impossible to rally them."

- Colonel George Washington
Excerpt from a letter Washington sent to his mother, Mary Washington, about Braddock's Defeat. [30]

July 13, 1755, in Allegheny County, during the French and Indian War, General Braddock embarked on a mission to take the French fort of Duquesne. Before reaching the fort, Braddock and his men were attacked at the Battle of Monongahela. The names may not be memorable to most, but I do remember hearing the story of the battle when I was in elementary school. I remember it because of the remarkability of the tale. Because, despite having two horses shot out from under him during the battle, our young, future president, George Washington, came out of the battle without a scratch, despite also having four bullet holes in his coat.

The above quote by Washington is a recount of the battle, with a clear conclusion that the British were not the victors. In fact, this was the greatest British defeat in the 1700s. Keep in mind that Washington was still on the side of the British at this time.

As for the sixty-year-old General Braddock, he did not survive the battle. He was buried near the Great Meadow that is a part of Fort Necessity. The location of his grave was chosen in an area where it was hoped that the general's resting place would not be disturbed; and there it still remains. [31]

To be fair, there are no known reports of hauntings or ghosts in the area of Braddock's defeat and grave. This does not mean that there is no

---

[30] Washington, George. "Braddock's Defeat, July 18th, 1755." *National Center.* 6 June. 2011. Web. <www.nationalcenter.org/Braddock'sDefeat.html>.

[31] "The Battle of Monongahela 1755- Braddock's Defeat." *British Battles.* 1 Jan. 2010. Web. 16 May 2011. <www.britishbattles.com/braddock.htm>.

paranormal activity there; just that nothing has been documented yet. Ghosts or not, the location is a part of the history of not only Pennsylvania, but also of the United States. Considering that it is a small portion of a reportedly haunted area, it may well be worth a visit to this location as well.

Directions: US 40 (11 miles east of Uniontown, PA and 1 mile west of Farmington, PA).

GETTYSBURG
(ADAMS COUNTY)

Over a stretch of three days of battle, the Union (North) and Confederate (South) clashed in a sea of bloody tides. Acres of Pennsylvania farmland were stained red with blood, the scent of death perfuming the air for months after the battle was over. Beneath our Northern soil, thousands of men were buried; some without a name and an unaccountable number of whom considered the land to be enemy territory.

"While his body lies beneath the enemies soil at Gettysburg, we hope his spirit has passed to a better world where no enemy can hurt him again."

- Isaac M. Hite, Private in the Army of Northern Virginia [32]

---

[32] Coco, Gregory A. *Confederate Killed In Action at Gettysburg*. Gettysburg: Thomas Publications, 2001. Print. 63

Gettysburg is considered by many to be the most haunted place in the United States. Hundreds of encounters and stories have been told and documented over the past century, ever since the battle ended. With a grand total of 51,000 causalities, there are plenty of ghost stories; some of which have yet to be told.

Author's note: This place offers quite an opportunity for paranormal investigators. Despite the many tragic deaths, unlike other places with excessive tragedies, Gettysburg is a place where I never felt unwelcomed, afraid, or paranoid during the day or night. The unknown can be scary and there are ghosts and inhuman entities out there that can be unpredictable; but even with eth burden of such tragedy, this is one place that does not feel cursed by it.

Day 1 – July 1st, 1863 Locations

Oak Hill

It was a cool evening in March of 2010, three friends chatted amiably while sitting on the walls around the Eternal Light Peace Memorial. They spoke of the battle, the soldiers and, of course, the ghosts. Taking turns in the growing darkness to walk alone around the memorial and up a little trial behind it that led to a bare spot with new trees and no memorial stones. Being not yet spring, the area was not overgrown with the green brush that usually crowds beside the trails.

One of the females had gone first, she did not see or hear anything unusual; nevertheless, she had the feeling that she was being observed by someone. The male in the group went second, taking the path up the little hill. As the two women sat on the wall watching the direction he had gone in, they noticed the shadowy figure of a man standing on the hill near the bare area. He looked as though he was wearing an officer's hat. As they watched him, they saw that he was pointing towards Iverson's Pits and then he started walking down the hill towards the Pits. Thinking it was their friend pointing something out to them, they turned to look in that direction. Seeing nothing, they turned back to find their friend coming towards them from the bottom of the trail. The shadowy figure had been walking away from them in the opposite direction. Giving the time and direction difference between the two, the women could not believe that their companion and the shadow could have been the same person. There were no other cars or people in the area to add any credence to the idea that the figure was of this world.

Having a soldier overlooking that area could be quite possible. A number of men had died in the field area of the Pits; their deaths came so fast that many were caught together in their line formations. The area of Oak Hill is not a place that most people would know by name. That is because the area is better known by the monument that stands on its hallowed ground, the Eternal Light Peace Memorial.

Investigation May 15th, 2011

5:07:01 p.m. – Investigator speaking to a fellow investigator – "Is Little Round Top over that way?"

5:07:06 p.m. – DRR – "Yes" – male voice.

Day 2 – July 2ⁿᵈ, 1863 Locations

Devils Den

In the early morning hours of a cold, wintry December day, I and a friend began our first scientific based investigation and conversation with the dearly departed. Of all the areas in Central Pennsylvania, Gettysburg seemed to be the best to test our new equipment. Despite the heavy fighting and numerous soldiers that passed through the den on their way to their deaths, this area of the battlefield is relatively quiet when it comes to the paranormal.

At a small corner of the bolder mass, we received our first EVP on the digital recorder. Because of the scratchiness of the white noise, the wave lengths in which spirits sometimes speak, the young soldier's name was inaudible. When asked his age, he responded with, "twenty-four, give or take." Afterwards, the area grew silent again. A young age to be fated to eternity on the other side; yet, despite his early death, the fact that he was pleasant and willing to communicate with us, spoke volumes for the young man who has yet to be named.

"Sharp shooters" spot at Devil's Den

Only one other ghost communicated with us in the den area. He was near the parking lot in the front of the den; popping into our conversation about visiting the Wheatfield, and telling us not to go there. His voice sounded much older and huskier than the guest of our previous exchange. Whether it was because he knew of the carnage in that field and the danger that once waited there; or because he did not want us to leave yet is unknown, for afterwards he grew silent as well. It can take a lot of energy for the dead to try to communicate with the living; many times, we are left with only pieces of conversations and sentences. It is not always an ideal circumstance, though every little bit helps when giving these men a name and assistance to find peace.

"We were ordered forward, and advanced a distance of one mile over a very rough and rugged road – the worst cliffs of rocks there could have been traveled over."

- Official report – Colonel James Sheffield, 48th Alabama; General Law's Brigade. [33]

Devils Den is truly and amazing canvas of earthly formations. Below the watchful eyes of Little Round Top, a treacherous expanse of large boulders and stones lie as if they were placed there by unnatural forces; a puzzle of pieces piled together with little shadowy crevices where men crawled to hide from the torturous sun above, and the hail of bullets surrounding them. The wounded and frightened were both seeking the same refuge, together where some may still be seeking their escape from the battle outside. Unlike some other places on the battlefield, such as the Slaughter Pen and the Valley of Death, which earned their names because of the battle; the den came upon the its name years before the war. Although, no one knows for sure how or when it received such an ominous title; whether through tall tales or because of a Native American battle that happened long before the Civil War, the land has certainly lived up to the designation. However the name came to be, with having such a moniker,

---

[33] Coco, Gregory A. *Confederate Killed In Action at Gettysburg.* Gettysburg: Thomas Publications, 2001. Print. 99

there is probably a good chance that there are more than only Civil War soldiers wanderings through the rocks, nearby stream, and the valley that has become overwhelmingly associated with death and blood.

Little Round Top

"Bayonets!" The command was shouted down the ranks of the 20ᵗʰ Maine. Bayonets or death was the unspoken acknowledgment.. The young soldier glanced at his commander Colonel Joshua L. Chamberlain, gauging his reaction. Against the unfathomable odds and facing the cold steel of an enemy (an army created using friends, relatives, and schoolmates) his commander stood unflinching. Splinters of tree bark fluttered into his face as a mini ball barely missed him. Transporting the young man back to the reality of the moment, he pulled the sharp bayonet from its casing, mounting it on his musket.

"The rebs must be getting tired," said the older soldier next to him, his scruffy beard black from biting the gun powder packets. Nodding at his comrade, the younger reclined against the tree where the splinters had spawned; exhaling a deep breath. Watching as the line of men down from him stood in attention, preparing to charge. On unsteady legs he rose with them. His heart beating faster as the rushes of adrenaline coursed through his mortal body. He took another deep breath, putting all his weight on his right leg, preparing for the race down the hill.

The command was quick, sharp, and loud, "charge!" In one fluid motion, the line of blue moved down the hill.

~*~

Strange tales have been woven into this little battle ravaged hill. When asked about their experiences on the battlefield, a group of friends told the story of something that happened to them while visiting the location of Colonel Chamberlain's famous charge.

The charge made quite a mark on history, with the commander of the 20th Maine being faced with the possible annihilation of his regiment and the Union army as well since the regiment was the flank; he ordered an unprecedented bayonet charge down the hill into the oncoming enemy. Many factors played into Chamberlain's decision: the fact that the Southerners were exhausted from the long march into Gettysburg followed by repeated charges up the Little Round Top; and that each man in his regiment had little to no ammunition left. [34]

Down the line from the Maine men, the 83rd Pennsylvania, 44th New York, and 16th Michigan were facing the rest of General Hood's Division of the 4th and 5th Texas, and the 4th and 47th Alabama regiments. [35]

What did the friends see while in this area of the battlefield? It has been retold for years that a "vortex" is on the hill that enables ghosts and spirits to move about freely to and from the area. What the friends saw was not a human though, it was a black cat. As superstitious and peculiar as that may sound, it is interesting to note that during the Civil War at Fort McAllister in Savannah, Georgia, the men had a black cat mascot for the fort.

Perhaps the vortex at Little Round Top could enable spirits to travel in an even more unexpected way than only between our world and the next. Maybe time is elusive in these circumstances and the history and modern times are one.

Investigation March 30th, 2012,

3:13:20 p.m. – Investigator – "What is your name?"

3:13:26 p.m. – Spirit Box – "E___."

3:30:10 p.m. – Investigator – "Are you a part of the 20th Maine?"

3:30:15 p.m. – Spirit Box – "Yes."

---

[34] "The 20th Maine & 15th Alabama at Little Round Top." *Brother's War*. 2 April. 2011. Web. 2 April. 2011. <http://www.brotherswar.com/Gettysburg-2e.htm>.

[35] Brann, James R. "Defense of Little Round Top." *America's Civil War* 1 Nov. 1999. Print.

Investigation April 1st, 2010

EVP Session taken while walking up the hill from Plum Run near Devils Den to the top of Little Round Top.

* By Plum Run

7:55 p.m. – Digital Recorder – Whispering.

7:56 p.m. – Investigator – Hears an electric sound.

7:57 p.m. – Two investigators – Hear a noise.

7:59 p.m. – Investigator – Sees a blue light.

8:00 p.m. – Digital Recorder – Inaudible words.

8:01 p.m. – Investigator – Sees a face poking out from between two rocks near the top of Little Round Top.

* About halfway up the hill, walking alongside the road.

8:02 p.m. – Investigator – Felt like someone was walking next to her.

8:02 p.m. – Investigator – Sees two flashes of light near the top of the hill.

8:03 p.m. –Investigator – Hears footsteps.

8:05 p.m. – Digital Recorder – "Get to the ground!" – male voice.

8:06 p.m. – Investigator – Sees shadowy movement, as if someone is crouching down and looking around. There was some white mist around the figure.

8:07 p.m. – Investigator –Hears footsteps and has a pain in her neck.

8:08 p.m. – Investigator – Feels a pain in her abdomen, right lower quadrant.

8:08 p.m. – Investigator – Feels a cold spot.

8:08 p.m. – Investigator – "I have a pain in my right side."

8:08 p.m. – Digital Recorder – "I hurt you" – male voice.

8:09 p.m. – Digital Recorder – "Hello" – male voice that is different from the previous voice.

8:09 p.m. – Investigator – Sees shadowy feet marching.

8:10 p.m. – Digital Recorder – Disembodied gun shot.

8:10 p.m. – Investigator – "I see shadows and like someone is down there."

8:10 p.m. – Digital Recorder – "Like me?"

8:11 p.m. – Investigator – Sees a shadow.

8:13 p.m. – Digital Recorder – "Help me!" – male voice.

8:17 p.m. – Investigator – "Are you part of Hood's Division?"

8:17 p.m. – Digital Recorder – "Help me!" – male voice.

8:29 p.m. – Investigator – Is getting a headache*

Just like other places in the park, the cries of "help me" still ring through time.

* Headaches can be a physical sign that a strong paranormal or electromagnetic field is near the person.

The battlefield has been untouched by war for over a century; yet it seems that the men who fought and died on Little Round Top still hold strongly to their post at the end of the Union line, the flank, the anchor of the Northern Army.

Triangular Field

October 16, 2010

11:36:24 a.m. – Investigator – female investigator feels hair pulled.

11:36:50 a.m. – Investigators – hear whispering, no EVPs on the digital recorder.

11:38:25 a.m. – Investigators – hear footsteps, no EVPs on the digital recorder.

11:43:26 a.m. – Investigator –sees movement out of the corner of her eye.

11:43:30 a.m. – Investigator – "What is your name?"

11:43:34 a.m. – Digital Recorder – Unreadable answer.

11:46:04 a.m. – Digital Recorder – Painful yell.

11:56:24 a.m. – Digital Recorder – "Come here!"

Just beyond the Devil's Den, behind the rocky formation (if you view the front as the area where the parking lot is located), lies the Triangular Field. Best known as the area where technology is not welcome: cameras fail, batteries are drained, and other technical issues arise. Quite a few avid Gettysburg ghost hunters will tell you that if you value your expensive equipment, do not take it into this field.

There are various reasons why these failures can happen; the common answer being that ghosts drain electrical equipment for "food" or energy to help them manifest. Being that the Triangular Field has no such sources for the spirits to normally feed from, they find other ways to strengthen their communication with the living.

That may not be the only reason that they seem to dislike cameras and the like. Near the Triangular Field is Devil's Den, where the body of a soldier was supposedly moved from where he died and positioned for a photograph. This photograph is better known as the "sharp shooter" was taken in-between the rocky configuration near the field. Perhaps these spirits saw what happened and considered it a sign of disrespect. Though that is only an assumption of what could be. This type of posing may have happened on more than one location; but that we may never know the whole truth for sure.

Respectful treatment of the dead is a part of society and of paranormal investigator; to not follow this rule of etiquette may cause rifts between the spirit world and ours. It may also stir unwanted attention and negative activity.

Wheatfield

A whirlpool that is how veterans of the battle at the Wheatfield described the scene, the field's once golden wheat trampled down and soaked with human blood. Within one day, the nineteen acres that encompasses the field changed hands six times.

Union troops under the command of Brigadier General Regis de Trobriand held the ground first, with men positioned smartly behind the stonewall at the end of the field. Charging through the woods on the other side of the field, where the marching can still be heard today, advanced Brigadier General George Anderson's Georgia brigade.

Just like the scenario that played out for the men on Little Round Top, both Union and Confederate troops were running low on ammunition. To conserve what was left, though it was a costly and dangerous maneuver, Anderson lined his men directly in front of the stonewall and ordered the men to go forward.

As the ammunition ran lower, the Union decided to retreat away from the wall, leaving it clear for a Confederate siege. Suddenly, in an effort to retrieve their lost, precious ground, the Union turned around in a bayonet charge, reclaiming their stony holding just in time for reinforcements for both sides to arrive. Coming from between the buildings of the Rose Farm, emerged General Joseph B. Kershaw and his South Carolina brigade.

I rallied the remainder of my brigade and Semines's at Rose's...That night we occupied the ground over which we had fought, with my left at the Peach Orchard, on the hill, and gathered the dead and wounded — a long list of brave and efficient officers and men. Captain Cunningham's company of the 2nd Regiment was reported to have gone into action with forty men, of whom but four remained unhurt to bury their fallen comrades. My losses exceeded 600 men killed and wounded, - about one-half the force engaged.

- Brig. General Joseph Kershaw, C.S.A. [36]

Eye witness accounts are rarely unbiased and give only one side to an event, how the speaker sees it. Two different people can see the same event and recount two different stories. Even dates and the numbers of the dead can be off. Documents can list an account of dead, wounded, and missing. Although is missing really an accurate description for those men who are missing in this world but were probably wandering through the next?

March 1st, 2010

2:12:53 p.m. – Digital Recorder – "There's a house." – male voice.

2:20:54 p.m. – Investigator – "Did you want to fight in the war?"

2:20:59 p.m. – Digital Recorder – "Yes." – male voice.

October 16th, 2010

2:30:31 p.m. – Digital Recorder – Loud bang.

2:32:00 p.m. – Digital Recorder – Muffled whisper.

2:34:14 p.m. – Investigator – "Can I sit on this rock with you?"

2:34:36 p.m. – Digital Recorder – "Hello" – male voice.

2:35:53 p.m. – Investigator – "I heard, the last time we were here, somebody talking about a house and a barn on the other side of the trees. Were you going to the house?"

2:36:53 p.m. – Digital Recorder – "There was a house" – male voice.

2:38:56 p.m. – Investigator – "I would like to ask you again what your name is?"

---

[36] "Kershaw's Brigade at Gettysburg." *Civil War Reference*. 1 Jan. 2011. Web. 2 Apr. 2011. <www.civilwarreference.com/articles/detail.php?article=120>.

2:40:53 p.m. – Digital Recorder – "Hello" – male voice.

The house that is spoken of is undoubtedly the Rose Farm house. John Howard Wert, a local citizen and teacher remarked upon the farm following the battle; stating that:

> *In the garden of the Rose house in full view,…nearly one hundred rebels were buried. All around the barn, even within the house yards, within a few feet of the doors, were in numbers, the scantily buried followers of the Confederate cause. Two hundred and seventy-five were buried behind the barn; a rebel colonel was buried within a yard of the kitchen door.*[37]

On a random trip through Gettysburg in March of 2012, two of us stopped by the Wheatfield again, taking with us only the spirit box to see if we could have a real time conversation on the sacred ground. For the most part, the ghosts were quiet; however, one did give us his name, "Captain Stewart." There were a number of regiments that he could have belonged to and I have yet to find any traces of a Captain Stewart thus far. Perhaps someone else will be able to find out the rest of his story.

---

[37] Coco, Gregory A. *Confederate Killed In Action at Gettysburg.* Gettysburg: Thomas Publications, 2001. 63. Print.

Day 3 - July 3rd, 1863 Location

Pickett's Charge

Thick, heavy, and unrelenting hot for the men in their heavy cotton uniforms; the summer weather was a torturous field taunting with only the slightest warm breezes blowing past the trees. A mix matched canvas of grays, browns, and the occasional spots of blue, lined the front of the full, green trees. Indomitable spirits in tattered uniforms.

With the rat tat tat of the snare drums, the line began to march forward; the men side by side as brotherly comrades; the starred blue 'x' of the Confederate banner leading the way. Cannon shells blasted overheard, the soldiers paying little heed to the artillery bombardment that started hours earlier. Fate and the 'Angel of Death' marching in stride with the soldiers as the distance between the men and their finish line, at the clump of trees of the Union line, shrank.

Cannon shells blasted overhead again, knocking holes in the formations as a few shells fell into their targets. Here and there, a man would look back at his fallen comrades whose blood now stained his uniform. Ahead of them, the red, white, and blue stars and stripes of the Federal Flag blew. Closer to their mark, the Union line across from them opened fire in a volley of poisonous lead.

"Forward!" the command rang out.
"Charge!" another command was shouted.

In the hopelessness of the moment, regiments and divisions began to turn back; retreating to their own side of the field. While Pickett's generals: Lewis Armistead, Richard Garnett, and James Kemper continued to lead their Virginians to the line. In a round of musket and cannon fire, Garnett and Kemper fell, one wounded and one presumably dead. Armistead was the only general to climb over the stonewall; only to be shot as well.

Men lay dying on the field, knowing that their end was coming as their life blood flowed from their bodies. In the stagnant heat, some wished for death to come and end their pain. Other's wished for the battle to end in victory; and the rest wanted to be saved.

Three divisions numbering roughly between 12,500 and 15,000 soldiers, depending on which account one reads, crossed the treacherous mile of open field. Within an hour, half of this number was dead, dying, wounded, or captured.

March 14th, 2010

- Confederate side of the line.

8:45:10 a.m. – Investigator – Hears a man's voice.
9:20:15 a.m. – Investigator – "What is your name?"
9:21:02 a.m. – Digital Recorder – "Anderson."

October 16th, 2010

- Union side of the line.
6:12:24 p.m. – Investigator – "Were you with Armistead?"
6:12:27 p.m. – Digital Recorder – "Yes."

May 15th, 2011

- Union side of the line.

5:31:41 p.m. – Investigator – "Does anybody here know the whereabouts of General Garnett's body or what happened to him?"
5:32:04 p.m. – Digital Recorder – "I know."

General Richard Garnett, against General Lee's orders, rode his horse during the charge. It was either ride or not be in the fight at all due to a wounded leg. Courageously, he drove his men forward until he was shot from his horse within sixty yards of the stonewall. His body was never identified.

The other divisions involved in the charge were commanded by Brigadier General J. Johnston Pettigrew and Major General Isaac R. Trimble. The corps commanders were Lieutenant General James Longstreet, with his First Corps, and Lieutenant General A. P. Hill's Third Corps. Their ranks made of brave men from Virginia, Tennessee, North Carolina, Mississippi, and Alabama.

At 2 p.m. the charge began, the goal being to reach and cross the Union line, the intended sight, a clump of trees at what is known as "The Angle." At the same time, a Confederate Calvary under the orders of J.E.B. Stuart would circle around behind the Union line, thereby surrounding the Union at the center of the battlefield. The attack was a surprise to the Union Yankees; with the blazing summer heat; many thought they might have a day of reprieve from the fighting. Since both sides of their line had already been attacked, the middle of it seemed the safest place at that time.

The end of the battle came quickly; the wounded and surviving Confederates retreated back to their side of the field. Those who did not make it back to the line, either lay dead or dying on the fields of Gettysburg or were already in the hands of the Union Army. General Lee made the orders to retreat after the failed charge and on July 4th, the Army of Northern Virginia made its way back across the Mason Dixon line into the South.

If J.E.B. Stuart's Calvary would not have been cut off en route, the battle of Gettysburg may have had a different conclusion.

* To break the infantry down, from largest to smallest: Corps, Division, Brigade, and then Regiment. Several regiments make a brigade, several brigades a division, and several divisions make a corps.

October 16th, 2010

- Union Line of Pickett's Charge

6:00:45 p.m. – EMF – brief EMF spike.

6:12:06 p.m. - Investigator – "What is your name?"

6:15:28 p.m. – Investigator – "Anything else?"

6:15:30 p.m. – Digital Recorder – "Yes" – male voice.

6:18:44 p.m. – Digital Recorder – "Hey, get back here!" – male voice.

6:18:56 p.m. – Digital Recorder – "Hey!" – male voice.

6:18:58 p.m. – Equipment – Equipment malfunction – the digital recorder screen went blank, flashed the words 'one sec' and then went back to normal.

6:19:46 p.m. – Digital Recorder – "Help!" – male voice.

May 15th, 2011

- At the Angle

5:33:07 p.m. – Digital Recorder – "Hey" – male voice.
5:34:26 p.m. – Digital Recorder – "Mommy" – young male voice.

- Walking towards the old cyclorama.

5:35:54 p.m. – Digital Recorder – "Come here." – male voice.
5:37:45 p.m. – Digital Recorder – Deep exhaling breath.

5:39:05 p.m. – Digital Recorder – "Help me" – male voice.
5:39:35 p.m. – Digital Recorder – "(Hear or Help) me" – male voice.

- Walking away from the cyclorama.

5:39:42 p.m. – Digital Recorder – "Hey, it's (me or Meade)" – male voice.

"Well, it is all over now. The battle is lost, and many of us are prisoners, many are dead, many wounded, bleeding and dying. Your Soldier lives and mourns and but for you, my darling, he would rather, a million times rather, be back there with his dead, to sleep for all time in an unknown grave."
Major General George Pickett, CSA, to his fiancée, July 4th, 1863

Directions: Baltimore Pike, Gettysburg

GRAEME PARK
(MONTGOMERY COUNTY)

Moonlight glistened on the rippling waters of the lake by Graeme mansion. Under the light of the evening sun, a figure is silhouetted in shadow. She stands beside the lake waiting for her lover they say. From out of the darkness a second shadowy figure appears and strolls towards her. They look at each other for a silent moment and then embrace. Just as soon as they appear together, the couple fades into the night.

Where life tore them apart, death has brought the lovers together again.

The Keith House at Graeme Park

The woman is believed to be Elizabeth Graeme, a lady who led a remarkable and interesting life for a colonial woman. She was a poet, a former betrothed to William Franklin, Benjamin's illegitimate son, and she is credited as the first woman in our country to host intellectual social parties, a reminiscent scene of the princess in her castle, who surrounded herself with some of the greatest minds of her time.

Her relationship with William was short lived due to differences in political views between her family and his. Eventually, she met someone else, a Scotsman by the name of Henry Ferguson.

A few years after her marriage to Ferguson, the American Revolution began changing their lives forever. Elizabeth's husband's loyalties remained sympathetic towards England, which meant near disaster for her. Because of her husband's views, she was also eyes with suspicion. After Henry tricked her into unwittingly delivering a letter to General George Washington asking him to surrender, she was also viewed as a traitor.

Ferguson left the country to return to his native land, leaving his wife alone and in a losing struggle to keep her home at Graeme Park. The home was confiscated because of her traitorous associations; it was not until 1781 that she was able to reclaim the mansion. She lost the property permanently in 1791 because of financial difficulties.

Elizabeth Graeme had loved the mansion that her father had bought. In death, she still haunts the home that was related to such grief in her life. It is believed that also in death, she has been reunited with her lost love. Many of those who have recounted this tale believe that the lost love is Henry Ferguson. I am inclined to prefer an idea that it is William. Both men caused her grief in very different ways. William's father separated the pair and sent William off to Europe, where he met his wife; breaking Elizabeth's heart. But Henry caused her to lose her family's legacy.

The mansion still stands in the park. It was built in the early 1700s by Provincial Governor Sir William Keith. After a conflict with the Penn family, Keith was forced to leave Pennsylvania. His home was purchased in 1739 by Dr. Thomas Graeme. His daughter Elizabeth inherited the property in 1772. When she was forced to sell the property in 1791 because of health reasons and debts, it was bought by her nephew Dr. William Smith. The property changed hands several times throughout the years, before becoming the property of the Commonwealth of Pennsylvania in 1958. [38]

---

[38] "History." *Friends of Graeme Park.* 1 Jan. 2012. Web. 10 Mar. 2012. <www.graemepark.org/>.

A few other spirits are said to haunt the property, Elizabeth's father for one, who died on the property of a heart attack. The second being a female servant of the household who legend says was killed by a Hessian soldier during the American Revolution. However, historical documents dispute the accuracy of that claim.

Directions: 859 County Line Road, Horsham

GRING'S MILL
(BERKS COUNTY)

Some women are born to be unlucky in love; destined to pick the wrong men. This is not to say that men do not find themselves in similar circumstances, they just seem less likely to linger on this plane of existence afterwards. There are many places around the world with the ghosts of women who were either jilted by their lovers and died of broken hearts, or ones who committed suicide because of the pain caused by a man, and then there are those who died by more nefarious means at the hands of men they had loved. Gring's Mill happens to have two who may well fit into these categories.

Mary had an unfaithful husband, as the first part of the story goes, and she found out about his infidelities; the blessing and the curse of "women's intuition." Taking the necklace he had given her for her birthday, she threw it, smashing it into a mirror; the glass shattered sending shards flying and hitting her. Fleeing the house, she ran to the Tulpehocken Creek that runs beside the mill and washed the blood from her arms. Her ghost has been seen along the watery banks of the creek continuing to wash away the blood; unfortunately, this is not where the story of Mary and her ghost ends. [39]

She divorced her unfaithful husband and remarried, thinking of putting her past behind her. It is said, though there are not any witnesses to this story that Mary awoke in the night to find her husband standing over

[39] "Gring's Mill." *Freedom's Corner Haunts & History*. 1 Jan. 2012. Web. 30 Jan. 2012. <https://sites.google.com/site/hauntsandhistory/freedom'scornerhaunts&history4>.

her with a knife. Running from her house, she ran into the mill, racing up the staircase towards the top. Once she reached the third level, the stairs gave way and she fell to the bottom floor, breaking her neck.

February 24th, 2012

4:44:20 p.m. – Investigator – "We are by the mill trying to contact Mary."

4:44:24 p.m. – Spirit Box – Female voice.

4:45:06 p.m. – Investigators – Hear screams inside the mill.

4:45:14 p.m. – Investigator – "Mary are you screaming?"

4:45:20 p.m. – Spirit Box – "No."

Upon arrival at the mill, I was not expecting to find any tracings of the story of Mary to be true. It seemed like a rumor, possibly to explain the sightings of a female ghost near the mill. Having responses from a woman near the location of the mill, who answered to the name Mary, made me rethink this possibility. Especially because Mary does not seem to be alone in her wanderings, after a scream is heard by the investigators, an angry male voice on the spirit box and digital recorder, he yells out the word, "b****." Is the angry husband still around wanting to kill Mary himself? Is he angry that she accidentally ended her own life? Or is there an entirely different scenario to this story?"

Whichever it is, the investigation seems to have reaffirmed the fact that all stories may have a hint of truth at the start.

Tow Path

The other ghost story at Gring's Mill is much more tragic and most unfortunately, completely true. Louisa Bissinger was also the victim of an unfaithful husband; this affair was not quite one like Mary's. It was more of a public spectacle with Louisa's husband openly courting another woman. In despair of her unhappy marriage and life, on August 17, 1875, Louisa took her three children: Mollie, Lillie, and Philip to Gring's Mill.

Walking along the tow path to Lock 49, she filled a picnic basket with rocks. At 5 p.m., tying the picnic basket to her waste, she picked up her three children and jumped into the creek. Louisa sank to the bottom, drowning herself, and unborn child.

A witness saw the other three children bobbing up and down in the water; since he could not swim, he ran back to the mill and a boat was launched to save the children. By the time the rescuers reached the lock, the children had drowned. [40]

Witnesses have seen the three children, ages nine, six, and three, walking along the tow path. Sometimes helping to collect the rocks that would unknowingly to them, lead to their deaths. They are dressed in homemade clothing and when they reach the area where they died, the ghosts just disappear.

February 24, 2012

2:02:1- p.m. – EMF – Spike that was at the height of a child, near the bridge.

2:14:26 p.m. –Spirit Box – "Jump" – female voice.

2:14:50 p.m. – Spirit Box – "Water" – female voice.

2:17:10 p.m. – Digital Recorder – "Hot."- female voice.

2:18:07 p.m. – Digital Recorder – "Get out of here!" – female voice.

2:19:23 p.m. – Spirit Box – "Help" – male voice.

2:19:44 p.m. – Spirit Box – "Help us" – child's voice.

2:20:21 p.m. – Spirit Box – muffled children's voices.

2:22:23 p.m. – Investigator – "Can you tell us what your names are?"

22:22:31 p.m. – Spirit Box – "Bert."

2:23:07 p.m. – Spirit Box – "Help"

2:23:10 p.m. – Spirit Box – "Liz" – female voice.

2:25:27 p.m. – Investigator – Hears footsteps on the path behind us.

---

[40] Youker, Darrin. "What's the Story behind Infamous 1875 Murder-suicide? Ask Youker." *The Reading Eagle.*
Http://readingeagle.com/mobile/article.aspx?id=259724., 28 Oct. 2010. Web. 30 Jan. 2012.

For several minutes, there is a back and forth between one of the investigators and a female spirit believed to be Louisa on the spirit box. Every time the investigator asked questions or brought up the tragic events of the children's deaths, there were responses on the spirit box. All of which were, sorry to say, unreadable.

Local medium Lisa Mansfield also had a conversation with Louisa Bissinger. This was Lisa's first investigation with the Black Moon Paranormal Society and she had this to say about her experience:

My experience at Gring's Mill was an interesting one. I definitely felt a dark presence due to the deaths that occurred there. The feeling was a bit overwhelming and made me feel a little dizzy and it made my head hurt. I felt the presence of Louisa Bissinger and her children; she is a very angry and dark spirit. Her children did not want to speak to me but I could feel their sadness. I also had a vision of Louisa in the water and she was following us as we walked the path.

Lisa added that Mrs. Bissinger's anger increased as the investigation questions became more emotionally probing and, she felt, accusing in regards to the deaths of her children.

By all accounts, Louisa does not feel responsible for the deaths. She blames her husband for everything that happened. These sentiments were not hers alone, at the time of the deaths, as the rumors came out about his infidelities; the once popular Captain Philip Bissinger began to lose public opinion in his favor. The restaurateur and eventual President of the Reading Brewing Company denied the allegations, only to have Louisa's brother come forward to support her conclusions; and to call her husband a murderer.

Louisa and her children are not the only ones who haunt the tow path by Lock 49. There were several recordings on the spirit box by women named Betsy and Ethel.

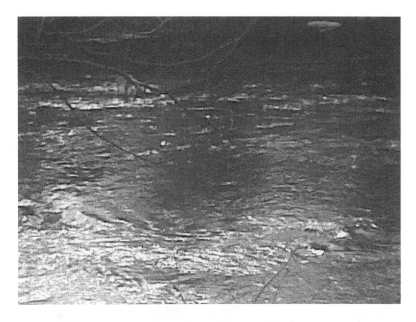

Two photos taken simultaneously at Gring's Mill where we made contact with Louisa Bissinger.

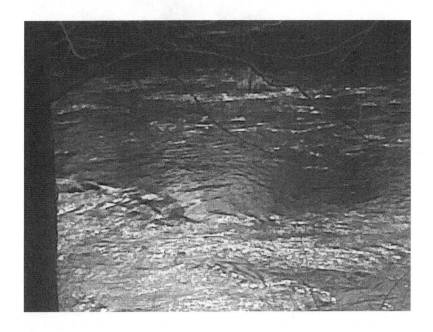

Hessian soldiers from the American Revolution are also still in the area. Local history states that a Hessian prisoner of war cemetery was located the confines of the park. These soldiers were German mercenaries, used during the Revolution by the British. The soldiers are more curious than anything else. Lisa saw two of them walking on the path towards us. Within the mix of German words that we were able to pick up, the clearest one was "bitte." Bitte can have several meanings but it's a polite word, usually meaning "please." When asked if anyone has any questions, a heavily accented "I do" was given in response; right before one of our bags fell off of a bench and on to the ground. Another heavily accented voice came through the spirit box asking, "What is that?" in regards to a cell phone that we were using to translate our words from English to German.

While Gring's Mill has an active haunted scene, it is probably best that those who are easily consumed by emotional and empathic energy do not visit such a mentally haunting site.

Gring's Mill

Directions: Off of 222, south if you are coming from Harrisburg and north if you are coming from Philadelphia. It is off of Tulpehocken Road.

HAWK MOUNTAIN SANCTUARY
(BERKS/SCHUYKILL COUNTIES)

Thunder clapped in the evening sky. Rain fluttered down, blocking out the sun, and growing increasingly vicious in its assault on the weary traveler. He peered through the graying mist before him, making out a small white house and farm in the distance, shelter against the darkening storm. Mud splattered his boots as he made his way to the inn; knocking on the door,

"Do you have a room for the night?"

"Of course, you poor soul! Come in! Tonight is not a night for the living to be out," cooed the middle-aged woman on the other side of the door.

The door slammed shut behind him as he stepped into the dimly lit house. A fire crackled in the hearth, barely warming the inn. It is still better than being outside, the traveler thought to himself.

"I must tend to the meal, my husband will show you to your room. He is gathering some firewood."

On cue, the front door blew open as a hooded figure stepped inside. Water dripped from his cloak, which he shook up while juggling the firewood that he carried in from the shed.

"Matthias, we have a guest."

"Welcome to our home, sir! I am Matthias and this is my wife Margaret. Take care and warm yourself by the fire."

Pulling off his own cloak and mud soaked boots; the traveler laid them on a hanger near the fire to dry. Holding on to the pouch he carried tightly against his body.

The evening meal finished brewing and the traveler, the inn keeper, and his wife sat around the rickety wooden table in a strange silence. After the bowls had been cleared, the mistress of the house brought out two mugs of beer. The visitor drank until the hour was late, trying to put the storm, his burdens, and the eeriness of the little cottage out of his mind. It is the storm; he thought to himself, the storm is what is making everything about this place feel so dark. So consumed was he trying to control his wayward thoughts that he never noticed that the inn keeper only casually sipped on his mug throughout the evening.

Matthais yawned loudly, "Best time to turn in lad, here let me help you to your room."

"I can manage, thank you," the man replied gruffly.

He walked in the room, closing the door behind him and collapsed on the bed, still clutching his pack close to him. Within a few minutes, his breathing slowed, shortened by the loud snores vibrating from his throat.

Hours passed in the night, until the light of a single candle shone under the door outside of the room. Quietly, and gradually, the door was pushed open. Peering inside the innkeeper looked around the room, noting the location of the traveler and his belongings. With a huff, he blew out the candle.

~*~

Dawn was approaching quickly in the light gray sky; the moon bowing to the rising sun. Matthais carried his shovel back to the barn, stepping out from inside, he wiped his hands. Returning to the house, he pulled off his boots and sat them next to the other set by the fire.

Turning to his wife he asked, "How much did he leave us?"

"Enough to cover our troubles. Mayhap you can put the boots and cloak to good use?"

"It is a poor material, but it will do for now."

Life in the innkeeper's house continued on its usual path throughout the day. His wife made the meals and straightened up the bedrooms; Matthias went to the barn to clean. The busy day began to change into night, the moon replacing the sun in their continual dance across the sky. Just as the last rays of the sun set, there was another knock at the day.

~*~

March 24th, 2012

Start time of investigation: 2:25 p.m.

3:10:21 p.m. - Digital Recorder - "Knife used."

3:10:27 p.m. - Digital Recorder - "Death."

3:12:10 p.m. - Investigator - "What were you killed with?"

3:12:16 p.m. - Digital Recorder - "A knife."

3:14:20 p.m. - Digital Recorder - "Woman."

Matthias Schambacher's, the innkeeper, grave lies in New Bethel Cemetery; establishing at least proof of his existence. On his deathbed, they say he confessed to killing eleven people in order to rob them of their belongings. [41]

March 24th, 2012

3:19:10 p.m. - Investigator - "Are you the innkeeper?"

3:19:18 p.m. - Digital Recorder - "No!"

---

[41] Huesken Jr., Gerald. "Strange Case of Hawk Mountain and Matthias Schambacher." *Examiner.* 25 Oct. 2010. Web. 30 Jan. 2012. <article/the-strange-case-of-hawk-mountain-and-matthias-schambacher>

3:21:20 p..m. - Investigator - "What is your name?"

3:21:29 p.m. - Digital Recorder - "Mister."

3:22:40 p.m. - Investigator - "Say your name."

3:22:47 p.m. - Digital Recorder - "Asner."

3:26:12 p.m. - Investigator - "Is your name Matthias?"

3:26:34 p.m. - Digital Recorder - "No"

3:28:14 p.m. - Investigator - "Were you a victim?"

3:28:20 p.m. - Digital Recorder - "Victim"

~*~

Cursed seems to be the most accurate way to describe Hawk Mountain. Similar to Chickies Rock, Hawk Mountain has tales of bad blood between the settlers and natives, death, and numerous recorded hauntings.

The ghostly, dark tales begin in the year 1756, four years after the founding of Berks County. A family by the name of Gerhardt lived in the mountain area. In February of 1756, the family home was attacked by Native Americans, and the family murdered, save for one. Somehow, the young, eleven-year-old Jacob Gerhardt managed to escape into the woods and survive. After the murders, he was taken in and raised by neighbors. His life was never the same, and he was haunted by the memory of that February night until the day he died. For some inexplicable reason, he returned to the area where his family home had been; he built a new home and remained there until the end of his life.

In the 1800s, Matthias Schambacher bought the property and supposedly murdered eleven people. So far there seems very little reason to consider the land to be cursed, a serial killer is rare, to be sure, but what else? Massacres between the Native Americans and the settlers were rather frequent in the 16 and 1700s. Now is the part where the stories start becoming a little odder. For instance, when Matthias confessed on his death bed to the murders, he said that he committed them because voices coming from the woods told him to kill those people. He also stated that the area is home to a great evil.

Then, after the death of that Matthias, another man of the same first name came to this place. This Matthias was a devout Catholic, a preacher, a good man by all accounts, who came to fight the evil of the mountain. One day, a few of the locals came to the house to find that Matthias was gone. His door had been ripped off its hinges. Several days later, his mangled body was found in the woods.

From these experiences, numerous ghosts have gathered to support the tales. The Gerhardt family is said to haunt the woods, along with the victims of the innkeeper. It is believed that the investigators made contact with at least one of Matthias' victims, as seen in the investigation segment of this chapter. In the woods at night, voices scream and wail. Glowing lights appear through the trees, sometimes stagnant, other times they can be seen bright and flashing before disappearing suddenly.

The lights and screams are all hearsay. Who is to say that these experiences do not resonate from the wind blowing through the trees or the animals that inhabit the forest? Full body apparitions have also been reportedly sighted in the forest and down along the road, frightening people who are driving past the sanctuary.

As for the house where the murders and other deaths happened, it still exists and is not immune to the hauntings. Animals are said to not go near the place. Footsteps can be heard, as if someone is eavesdropping on conversations and a strange wailing comes from within the house and the barn.

Besides these spirits, there is also one of a young German girl who is believed to haunt the information center and gift shop. Her death occurred from a fall down the stairs. She is deaf and mute, so trying to make contact is nearly impossible. Though, it is said that if one listens closely, they can hear the sound of a pennywhistle that she blows on every so often. Some have claimed to see her apparition, floating above the floor at the exact number of feet high that the floor was before the building was remodeled. [42]

~*~

One of the view points at Hawk Mountain.

No matter how many ghosts are in the area, it is truly a magnificent hiking ground; one with a wondrous, breath-taking view. It is important to remember that the sanctuary is no normal haunting ground, it is an animal sanctuary for the preservation of some of the beautiful wildlife in the state. Though it is open to the public during the day, radios are forbidden on the grounds, so no spirit boxes or walkie talkies here. There is certainly no

---

[42] "Hawk Mountain Sanctuary." *Freedom's Corner Haunts & History*. 1 Jan. 2012. Web. 30 Jan. 2012.
<https://sites.google.com/site/hauntsandhistory/freedom'scornerhaunts&history>.

trespassing after hours, and this stands true for most of the places in this book. Investigating the paranormal is a wonderful thing, but respect to the living cannot always be foregone in the quest for knowledge. A balance must be maintained.

Directions: 1700 Hawk Mountain Road, Kempton.

HORSESHOE CURVE, BENNINGTON CURVE, AND ALTOON
(BLAIR COUNTY)

Fog covered the train tracks, not for the first time, in the early morning hours of February 18th, 1947. Traveling down the Cresson Mountain downgrade, the speeding locomotive belonging to the Pennsylvania Railroad, headed towards the 180 degree angle at Horseshoe Curve. An hour behind, the engineers were pushing the speed at sixty-five miles per hour, rounding the bend at Bennington Curve, near the railroad ghost town of Bennington, a curve that was meant to not be taken at more than thirty miles per hour.

In the dense fog of that early winter morning, the large passenger train jumped the tracks, careening into Gum Tree Hollow. Pieces of the train disintegrated on impact, several passengers were tossed from their sleeping compartments, others were crushed where they slept, dying instantly.

I shone my flashlight inside and saw arms and legs sticking up. Some railroad workers with acetylene torches were cutting the wreckage to release the passengers who were pinned down. The injured were being carried away on stretchers...It was a pretty weird sight and made me feel shaky. My two brothers, who drove from Altoona with me, became so nervous they could hardly hold still.

-Tom Lynam (Altoona Photographer) [43]

Two hundred people were on board that train, a number that includes passengers, mail employees, and railroad employees; less than seventy

---

[43] McIlnay, Dennis. *The Wreck of the Red Arrow: An American Train Tragedy.* Seven Oaks, 2010. Print. 37

walked away physically unscathed. Twenty-four were dead, the rest wounded, as the clashing sounds of metal grinded to a halt, the cries of the living and wounded filled the air. By morning, rescuers and onlookers crowded the racks above and the hollow below. This wreck is known as the Red Arrow Train Wreck. [44]

A sudden, traumatic death sometimes leaves ghosts unable to realize that they are dead. For the victims, their families, and the responders to the scene, the sadness of that scene could not be stopped by time. Emotion can create an energy that leaves a lingering feeling in the air.

~*~

Horseshoe Curve, would have been the next curve on the Red Arrow's traveling path. A place where the Irishmen sing songs while working on the railroad, and the ghost of a woman stands in the mist and rain. She is said to be beautiful, a true Irishwoman haunting an area where only railroad workers should be seen. With her, carries the all too frequent tale of a young lady waiting and searching for her missing lover. In this story, her young Irishman love is murdered in a drunken barroom fight, an account that is believed to have never reached her ears.

Her sad story leaves out how she died, when, or why. No one yet has been able to ask her. The young lass is seen by a tunnel on the Altoona side of the curve when it rains, is misty, or snowing.

As for the town of Altoona, it is said to be one of the most haunted towns in Pennsylvania, shadowing only Gettysburg. From the historic society, throughout the streets, old homes, and train tracks, ghost stories abound. Far too many to name in one book, the Irish lass is just a glimpse into the other world that hazes over the town. Waiting for the next lost soul to wander into its midst.

---

[44] "Altoona, Pennsylvania, Horseshoe Curve Train Wreck February 18, 1947." *Gen Disasters*. 1 Jan. 2011. Web. 18 Apr. 2011.
<www.gendisasters.com/data1/pa/trains/altoona-trainwreckfeb1947.htm>.

LITTLE BUFFALO STATE PARK
(PERRY COUNTY)

"Stop!" A female voice screamed through the spirit box; the loudest I have ever heard on any piece of equipment, making the hair on the back of my neck rise up. I heeded her word, stopping in my tracks on the tiny foot bridge behind the heads towards a little stone building, behind the farmhouse.

"Why?" I asked. "Who are you?"

My reply was silence. Accepting a warning I felt was there, I walked back to the front of the farmhouse. One of the other investigators sat on the porch, his head in his hands, complaining of a sudden migraine headache. The atmosphere was heavy, the air thick. Even though it was unusually warm for a March day, brandishing on 81 degrees, it was not humid.

"Hello, is anyone there?" I inquired, holding out teh spirit box, with the idea that the answer would be "yes," considering our intuitive feelings about the area. Yes was my reply, this time the voice was a man.

Words started pouring through the device, "breath," and then "killed."

"Killed? Why?"

"Gambling."

"Help him," the female's voice called out again.

"What is your name?" Requested an investigator.

"John."

"Can you tell us your last name?"

"Smith."

"John Smith?" Why are you still here? What happened to you?"

"Murdered!"

Blue Ball Tavern

Pennsylvania has its share of peculiar and unforgettable names: Bird-In-Hand, Intercourse, and Blue Ball. Which is why, even though it has been closed since 1841, this tavern is not a name easily lost in time. The Blue Ball Tavern, not to be confused with the Blue Ball Tavern and Inn in Baylesford, Pa; which was run by the notorious Prissy Robinson and is rumored to be haunted by Prissy and her supposed victims, opened in 1811 courtesy of John Koch. Who was one of the first farmers in the area.

Like other colonial taverns, Koch's tavern became a gathering place for locals and for travelers on the move between Carlisle and Sunbury on the Carlisle Pike. Also, reminiscent of other taverns, any number of activities would have gone on within: drinking, sharing of news, gossiping, resting, and maybe even a few illicit activities. History does not say for sure, and there is no in-depth history on this tavern in Perry County. Although rumors persist it was in that tavern that the plans for Perry County were created in 1821.

The farmhouse that currently stands on the site was built in 1865, using the foundation and pieces of the tavern in the construction. In the modern day, it serves as the Perry County Historical Society.

Shoaff's Mill

Following the walking trails past the haunted tavern, visitors come to Clay's covered bridge and Shoaff's Mill. The lingering spirit of a genteel voiced young woman greets the investigators. Other than greeting guests loud enough to be heard audibly and on the recorder, she remains otherwise quiet.

Questions were asked as to who she was, if she was connected to the beautiful historic house across the street that was owned by the owners of the mill. All the questions were met with silence and if not for a gently brush on the arms of the visitors, creating the feeling of cobwebs on the skin, we would have thought she had left.

Shoaff's Mill

On the trail behind the mill, the gruff, rough voice of a man can be heard mumbling inaudible words. Besides those places, most of the park was relatively inactive during the visit. Investigations were conducted near one of the lakes, at several points on a hiking trail that winds up the hill into the woods, and one was done by the covered bridge. No voices were picked up in any of those areas; there were no personal accounts, being touched or intuitive feelings. Regardless, Little Buffalo State Park still has some of the most beautiful hiking trails we have ever seen in our travels. So, despite the few voices, the trip proved worth the time to visit.

Directions: 1579 State Park Road, Newport

LORIMER PARK
(PHILADELPHIA COUNTY)

Bridge at Lorimer Park

An orange glow spread across the horizon before the dawn, banishing the night. Awoken from muted slumber, screams resonated in the fading night. Embers clicked and timbers cracked until breaking in a symphony chorus in the background of human cries of terror. It was a moment in time when it seemed as though the pits of hell were rising up to consume the earth. By daylight, the orchestra had diminished, and a once magnificent mansion estate had been turned to ash, never to be rebuilt.

Sometimes on winter nights, the smells of smoke, and the sound of horrible cries and screams, drift from where the mansion stood. A large stone marks where the Waterman mansion was in 1785. It is said that it burned down in the 1800s.

By day all seems quiet in the area, a paranoid feeling of being watched stems from the nearby woods. All the voices are silent; there are no screams, no remnants of the Waterman family still surveying the wreckage of their home. The world feels still and out of place in the area, stuck in a different time until you wander down the hill towards the water, heading to what is known as Council Rock.

Council Rock

The area known as Council Rock is believed by the locals to have been used as a meeting place for Native Americans; where the Lenni Lenape (Delaware tribe) would plan their activities and conduct rituals. The Delaware tribe was wide spread throughout eastern Pennsylvania and its neighboring states.

During the founding of Pennsylvania, William Penn made an effort to maintain peace between the Delaware tribe and the newly arriving colonists. While Penn made a name for himself as a tolerant and gifted leader, his endeavors increased the colonization of the state and put strain on the tribe. Eventually, the relationship between the two turned violent, with more of the Lenape dying by being killed by colonists after the French and Indian War, than those who died during the war. The Lenape first sided with the French but then allegiance to the British. Many of the tribe became part of Pontiac's Rebellion/War, which was an uprising of the natives in the state after the French and Indian War. Because of crowding and hostility during the first few centuries of tenure as a country, many members of the tribe left the country. Currently, what is left of the tribe lives primarily in Canada.

As for Council Rock, it is a magnificent natural stone wonder. Looking across the bank of the Pennypack Creek, several investigators thought that they saw movement and shadowy figures on the top of the rock where there was no one. Once again the feeling of being watched was strong with a hair raising paranoia. On top of the rock, one person heard the vibration of drumming. No one spoke to us, and besides the drumming, all was silent. However, silence does not mean alone.

After climbing on top of the rock, we hiked through the woods and then came back to the rock, trying an EVP session beneath the towering peak of the rock. The recorder picked up a back and forth conversation between two men that we could not understand.

It was during an investigation at Gettysburg that we learned that ghosts can use the spirit box to communicate with each other. How do we know? Because they were using it to talk to each other and, when asked if they liked using the box to talk to each other, we received a "yes." That conversation then continued with us just being causal listens and not really a part of the conversation. It is amazing what you can pick up unexpectedly.

There is another haunted spot within the park, this one we did not travel to see. Somewhere within the woods of Lorimer Park, is a stone triangle. People have come forward claiming to see the triangle encased in a red light sometimes at night, and feeling an eerie feeling. We cannot say whether or not the red light is an accurate or natural occurrence, however, eerie feelings seem to be the norm in this place.

Directions: Moredon Road, off of Huntingdon Pike (Rt. 232). It is located Huntingdon Valley.

MCCONNELL'S MILL
(LAWRENCE COUNTY)

Dangerous white water rapids crash in the Slippery Rock Creek, an area that has claimed many lives throughout time. Beside the creek, touching the land, another less obvious danger sits, an old mill. Originally built in 1852 by Daniel Kennedy, the mill had to be rebuilt in 1868, after a fire destroyed it. Thomas McConnell bought the location in 1875. The mill finally closed in 1928. [45]

Beside the mill, a path runs along the land, a trail that was once taken every day by an employee on his way to and from work. It was in the early morning hours of one of those regular working days that the man met a gruesome end, dying as a result of an accident with the mills machinery. It is said that piercing screams could be heard coming from inside the mill only minutes after the employee had shut the door.[46]

The story of the mill worker is by all accounts, just a story. Only legends and rumors mention the tale. There is another story involving the mill that holds a little more merit. The land is haunted by an old caretaker of the property, Moses Wharton. Known as "Old Mose," he was a freed slave from North Carolina who came to work at the mill in 1880. He passed away at a nursing home in 1954. His full body apparition is said to chase off unwelcome visitors, typically those who go after hours; carrying on his duty

---

[45] "McConnells Mills." *Western Pennsylvania Conservancy*. 1 Jan. 2011. 29 July 2012. <www.paconswerve.org/e-conserve/fall-07/30s.htm>

[46] "Best Pittsburgh Haunts." *CBS Pittsburgh*. 10 Nov. 2010. Web. 1 June 2011. <http://pittsburgh.cbslocal.com/top-lists/best-pittsburgh-haunts/>.

of maintain the property.

Near the mill, a covered bridge sits that was built in 1874. The ghost of a female child is purported to haunt this final location in the McConnell's Mill area. She is attached to the bridge due to a car accident at the site and she is only seen after a car passes through the bridge, when the driver looks in their rear-view mirrors. The bridge is still in use, therefore walking through it is not recommended, or else an unlucky person may find themselves joining the child in her haunting.

A location known as Hell's Hollow, with the Hell's Hollow falls is also nearby. It is a hiking trail that begins at the parking lot and crosses over Hell Run. It is supposedly not haunted, but with such an interesting name, who could resist a visit?

Directions: Off of Us-422 and Benjamin Franklin Highway

MOONSHINE CHURCH AND CEMETERY
(LEBANON COUNTY)

Out of the horrific tales in this book, none compare in terms to cold-hearted greed more so than the story that cursed the Moonshine Cemetery in Fort Indiantown Gap. The victim was not the subject of a passion murder, he was not killed in an accident or in combat; this man was simply unfortunate prey, entangled not by any of his own doing or knowledge, in a scam that would cost him his life.

This story begins in a small room of the Brandt Hotel in St. Joseph Springs, four men whispered together, plotting a plan of monetary gain.

"It is easy; we take out an insurance policy on the old man."

"What if we get caught?"

"We are not doing anything illegal."

"I am not convinced that the plan will work Henry."

"Don't be a coward!" scolded Israel.

"You need the money don't you?" asked George. "You are no better off than the rest of us!"

Josiah chimed in hesitantly, "What if he does not die as soon as we would hope?"

Henry thought for a moment, his thumb and index rubbing against his chin. "Then we hire someone to kill him."

"Shh! Lower your voice!" George reprimanded Henry. Leaning closer to the center

of the table, George's eyes took in the three men sitting with him. "I know who we could hire; it will be done quickly and quietly."

"We should wait for a bit before that, make it not seem so suspicious," suggested Josiah.

"Then it is agreed, ain't it? All three of you are with me on this? There is no turning back! Not one of us will be less guilty than the others," stated Henry. One by one, each man nodded his head in agreement. "We will meet with the old man tomorrow."

Four men planned the deed: Israel Brandt, Henry Wise, George Zechman, and Joshiah Hummel. The scheme was to take out a life insurance policy on sixty-five-year-old Joseph Raber, an act that was and is still legal. Raber was tricked into signing the papers by being told that the men wanted to help him. They wanted to ensure that his funeral expenses would be paid for and lessen the burden on others. Both Raber and his housekeeper, Polly Kreiser, survived off the charity of their neighbors.

As the months ticked by, the four determined that they could no longer wait for a natural death. They were in desperate need of money. On the afternoon of December 7, 1878, Brandt's neighbor Charles Drews and a local thief by the name of Frank Stichler, who was hired by Drews, went to see Raber. They asked if he would accompany them into town to Kreiser's Store. Drews and Stichler would later claim that Raber met with an accident, falling into the Indiantown Creek, where he would drown.

But as Benjamin Franklin wrote in *Poor Richard's Almanack*, "Three may keep a secret, if two of them are dead." It was not one of the four who reported the details of the conspiracy to the local authorities. In this turn of events, it was a man named Joseph Peters. Peters had been asked to take part in the venture by killing Raber and had turned the offer down. As a result of his report, the six men involved were arrested. It was during the trial that it was noticed that all six of the men had blue eyes; hence the name the Blue Eyed Six.

At the end of the trial all the defendants were found guilty of first degree murder. All six requested a new trial. George Zechman was the only one found not guilty. Some stories say that Brandt, Hummel, Wise, Drews, and Stichler were hanged. While other accounts state that Josiah Hummel died in prison before his execution date.

None of the Blue Eyed Six were buried in Moonshine Cemetery, which is only the resting place of their victim. Yet, reports say that haunting, glowing blue yes can be seen in the cemetery at night. Perhaps they are conjuring a new way to gain some comfort at the expense of Raber, who is also believed to haunt the cemetery. [47]

Besides the story of the Blue Eyed Six, according to local legends, Native Americans and a headless horseman also haunt the area of the Moonshine Church.

- To note: This area is private land and should NOT be visited at night. It is near the military base at Fort Indiantown Gap, and is patrolled by police and the military. I included the story only because it is a staple in the local ghost stories of the Central Pennsylvania area.

Directions: Route 443

---

[47] "Haunted Moonshine Church and the Blue Eyed Six." *Weird U.S.* 1 Jan. 2012. Web. 29 July 2012.
<www.weirdus.com/states/pennsylvania/local_legends/moonshine_church/index.php>.

PETER'S MOUNTAIN ROAD
(DAUPHIN COUNTY)

12:45 A.M., the clock glowed red on the cars dashboard as the driver sped up Peter's Mountain Road, climbing over Peter's Mountain. Rain was settling in, making fog roll down the mountain side. Headlights flashed on the asphalt, penetrating the fog, and glancing upon a pair of tan legs that were running along the road. The legs quickly faded into the fog before the full body apparition of a Native American appeared in the mist. He was crouched alongside the road, appearing to be searching the area for something, or someone. Before he too, disappeared into the haze.

Peter's Mountain is the large mountain behind the historic Peter Allen House, which was built in 1726 and is noted as the oldest house in Dauphin County. The house served as a stop on the old Sunbury Turnpike, and was built by its namesake, who was a trader and a surveyor. It is an elegant remnant of the pre-Revolutionary Pennsylvania frontier. The mountain crest overlooks the town of Halifax and a curve in the Susquehanna River. At the top of the mountain, a bridge runs above the road, connecting the top parts of the mountain; through which, one can hop on the Appalachian Trail.

Bridge at the Appalachian Trail on top of Peter's Mountain

The Appalachian Trial has both an interesting and a cryptic history. More than a few hikers have met their fates along the trial that runs from Georgia to Maine. Over the two thousand miles long path, hikers have been victims of accidents and murder. It seems like every state that the trail runs through, has a ghostly tale in relation to it. The nearby town of Duncannon is one of those stated sites where two hikers were murdered by a man named David Casey Horn, a bearded mountain man who was wanted by the FBI for murder. He was later apprehended in Harpers Ferry, West Virginia. His victims, Molly LaRue of Ohio and Geoffrey Hood of Tennessee, marked the sixth and seventh murder victims since the trail opened in 1925; their deaths occurred in 1990.

Considering how beautiful the trail is, and the number of people who have hiked it, do not let such tragic tales dissuade you have taking the trail. Accidents and danger can be found anywhere. With the amount of foot traffic there, the chances of becoming a victim are exceedingly slim. Please do take all the necessary pre-cautions if you do choose to go on a hike, whether it be the trail or elsewhere.

As for the Peter's Mountain side of the trail, there are no documented murder cases to speak however; the trail is not without a curious spirit. Besides the sightings of Native Americans on the mountain, the ghost of a man named Adam haunts the area around the parking lot at the top of the mountain. Adam did not say anything beyond his name. Leading one to wonder just why his spirit lingers on the trail. It makes one speculate where else a lonely or lost spirit can be found on certain sections of the trail.

Directions: Route 147 off of 322, near Harrisburg.

PINCHOT PARK
(YORK COUNTY)

In the early years of Pennsylvania's occupancy as a colony, and later a commonwealth, documentation of events: births, deaths, crimes, murders, burials, etc. were rarely and poorly recorded. Unwritten history has lain buried and hidden from the world for centuries, and finding these unwritten stories and answers is a part of investigating the paranormal.

Pinchot Park, the abbreviated name for Gifford Pinchot State Park in honor of Gifford Pinchot, a past governor of the state, is as quiet and relaxing an area as one could hope to find in Central Pennsylvania. Fishing, canoeing, Frisbee golf, boating, hiking, and camping-out in the beautiful scenic outdoors; it is hard to imagine that anything paranormal could be lurking in the green woods or near the sparking lake. Even with a few accidental drownings recorded in the lake, Pinchot Park seems nothing more than a recreation area by day. It is at night, and in the quieter times of the year, that a hidden element comes out.

During an investigation inside the park one afternoon, in the winter of 2010, myself and another investigator were walking along the frozen banks of Pinchot Lake. I was walking in the lead with her following behind me, when I heard the sound and sense that someone had fallen to the ground. Turning, expecting to see my teammate on the ground, I see her standing without a touch of snowy earth on her clothing. I asked if she almost fell, and she said, "no." Nor did she hear or feel the same sounds that I thought I did.

After returning home for the day and reviewing the evidence on the digital recorder, I did not hear anything that sounded like someone falling;

but before I asked the question, "did you fall?" a male voice comes across the recording saying, "help me."

Was this man a victim of accidental drowning? Or a companion of someone from a past era who met an untimely death in the area and he was hoping that someone could come and help his friend and the event continues to repeat itself? Perhaps he is a ghost from a time long before Pinchot even existed, the park not being dedicated until 1961.

Several years ago, during my college years, I lived in a house adjacent to the park property. During the day, the tree line created a beautiful encompassing view from the property. The sounds of nature emanated from the park, for anyone who loves the outdoors, it is really an exquisite sound. At night is when the feeling in the air was different and the view of the trees would send shivers down my spine.

Many of us have experienced the feeling of being watched, that primordial instinct that raises the hair on the back of the neck, alerting a person to danger or a nearby presence. By just closing your eyes when someone is near, the feeling can arise. As much as we sometimes like to pretend it is not there, we still have the intuition of our prehistoric ancestors. I could never discern who or, more appropriately "what," was watching from the woods, but I had no doubt that something was there. The night hides all things, living and dead.

It is not just within the park that visitors have had a variety of paranormal encounters. On Alpine Road in Wellsville, a drive that leads to several of the entrances to Pinchot, there is a small cemetery next to the road. Most of the names and dates have been rubbed off with time. The stone walls and tiny, old tombstones are usually hidden by untrimmed trees in the summer and snow in the winter, making it easy to drive by without noticing that a cemetery is there. Only after passing by the side do some visitors notice a black shadowy figure on a black horse in their rear view mirrors. He follows the cars for about half a mile before disappearing.

Alpine Road Cemetery

(Just to note, if anyone happens upon this cemetery, there is a small car pull off next to the location. Locals have warned visitors that the area is a popular nesting ground for venomous copperhead snakes.)

The occurrences may be few, yet with no written history giving any inkling that anything monumental happened in the area, one has to be curious as to what was the cause of the hauntings. Drownings may account for part of the activity; certainly it does not explain all. With sightings of shadows near the park, an eerie old cemetery, and feelings of paranoia where electromagnetic fields are non-existent, something is stirring the activity. This may be one of those times when a paranormal investigator may be lucky enough to discover a new history to the area; and once again change how people view the dead and what they have to offer us.

Directions: Rossville Road and Alpine Road, Wellsville

PINE GROVE FURNACE
(CUMBERLAND COUNTY)

Through a line of trees the car appeared, gray colored with a darkly tinted windshield and an unseen driver. For a mile or two it followed the car in front of it, keeping only a cars length between them. Then, as suddenly as it appeared, the car disappeared into another line of trees. Only slightly unnerved, the four friends continued on their way to the trail that would take them to Laurel Lake at Pine Grove State Park.

After spending a few enjoyable hours hiking around the lake, the friends decided to return home. Down the same long stretch of road, they drove on, surrounded by a lush green forest. A slight mist had begun to settle on the road, crawling between the trees. Reappearing again, just as instantly as it did the first time, that same gray car pulled behind them. It followed a few miles before, once again, turning off into the trees.

This may sound like an urban legend, but there are four witnesses that say it actually happened, those who were in the car being followed. They never did see who was driving the car, despite many other trips down to Pine Grove, they never saw it again.

The woods of Pine Grove have the characteristic of a Grimm Brother's fairytale, where children see fairies and adults hear the sounds of workers toiling away in a quarry that has long since been filled with water. That is quarry is Laurel Lake. My first investigative visit to the trails, recreation area, and park proved to me the truth of the sounds of the workers still mining the old quarry. Purely residual energy and the only EVPs I had on my digital recorder from this visit.

By the lake is a picnic area; down the road is the old iron furnace stack; as well as, the handsome iron masters mansion built by Peter Ege, and several other original buildings that were once a part of the iron furnace community.

Samuel Pope conveyed the land to George Stevenson way back in the 1700s. Eventually the furnace and surrounding lands came into the possession of Michael Ege, Joseph Thornburg and Thomas Thornburg in 1762. According to the deed, a furnace was already on the land at this time. Before Michael Ege passed away in 1815, he was listed as the sole owner of all the properties at Pine Grove, in addition to the Mt. Holly Estate Furnace and Cumberland Furnaces, which he divided between his children. His eldest son, Peter Ege, would take control of the Pine Grove Estate and he built a second furnace and the iron masters mansion; the mansion was for his wife Jane Arthur Ege. Peter lost the furnace at a sheriff's sale in 1838 to pay his numerous debts. Frederick Watts, the "Father of Penn State University," and Charles B. Penrose were the next owners of the Pine Grove properties. The South Mountain Iron Company took control in 1864. [48]

May 15th, 2011

* By the furnace

2:09:56 p.m. - Investigator - Hears a sound.

2:10:53 p.m. - Investigators - Feel a cold spot.

2:13:52 p.m. - Digital Recorder Response - "Why?" - male voice.

2:13:57 p.m. - Investigator - "How old are you?"

2:14:21 p.m. - Investigator - "What year is it?"

2:14:35 p.m. - Digital Recorder Response - "___44" - male voice.

---

[48] Greeley, Horace Andrew. "Recollections, Historical and Otherwise, Relating to Old Pine Grove Furnace." *PATC Archives*. 1 Jan. 2011. Web. 4 May 2011. <www.patc.us/history/archive/pine_grv.html>.

Pine Grove Furnace Stack

* At the Old Susquehanna Trail near the furnace.

2:49:50 p.m. - Digital Recorder Response - "Where are you going to eat?" - male voice.

2:53:35 p.m. - Investigator - Sees a young man running across the small stream, he was dressed in a blue jacket with red trim, it looked like an old military coat.

2:54:15 p.m. - Digital Recorder Response - "Hey" - male voice.

2:58:13 p.m. - Digital Recorder Response - "Hush" - male voice.

The most intriguing aspect of this investigation was the investigator seeing a full body apparition as he ran through the trees. It was only for a brief few seconds, but he seemed almost real. To add to the mystery of his appearance, I have not been able to find any historical documents that could contribute to a reason as to why a soldier, possibly from the American Revolution, would have been in that location. Most of the better known locations tied to the Revolution are closer to Philadelphia.

"The circle closed again directly, and the little folks went on singing and dancing with the wildest leaps...in a moment all had vanished, and the hill lay in solitude in the moonlight."

- Wilhelm and Jacob Grimm, The Little Folks' Presents

Directions: is located in Gardeners, PA

VALLEY FORGE
(CHESTER COUNTY)

I have just returned from spending a few days with the army. I found them employed in building little huts for their winter quarters. It was natural to expect that they wished for more comfortable accommodations, after the hardships of a most severe campaign; but I could discover nothing like a sigh of discontent at their situation... On the contrary, my ears were agreeably struck every evening, in riding through the camp, with a variety of military and patriotic songs and every countenance I saw, wore the appearance of cheerfulness or satisfaction.

- Anonymous Observer to the New Jersey Gazette December 25, 1777

Reconstructed huts at Valley Forge

Freedom is never free! This is a statement that has been repeated many times throughout history. There are those who have paid a price for the rest of the population. Some are still fighting, years, decades, and centuries after the wars have been waged.

April 29th, 2010

* Starting inside one of the reconstructed huts.

12:34:58 p.m. - Investigator - "Can you give us a sign that you are here?"

12:35:02 p.m. - Digital Recorder Response - "I'm here!"

12:51:10 p.m. - Investigator - "How long were you a member of the Continental Army."

12:51:14 p.m. - Digital Recorder Response - "I am."

Weary, and with the recent wounds from the Battle of Whitemarsh, Pennsylvania yet unhealed, George Washington's army marched to Valley Forge. Still holding tight to their fight for independence from the oppressive British monarchy, the army made camp for the winter of 1777. The poorly clad and ill-trained soldiers arrived on December 19th, so close to Christmas tide, yet most of them were far away from their families. Little concern for the dangers and sadness, they were determined to keep the war going even when the enemy changed from the British Empire to another danger closer to home, disease: dysentery, typhoid, and pneumonia, and starvation. Out of the 12,000 or more men camped at the forge, 2,000 would die. Two thirds of the dead passed away in the spring.

Their supplies were low, as they had been throughout the start of the war, and their little hovels that they had to live in were damp and disease festering. Many were left to sleep on wooden planks in their huts that they shared with twelve other men. [49]

---

[49] "The Encampment." *Valley Forge Legacy: The Muster Roll Project.* Friends of Valley Forge, 1 Jan. 2011. Web. 26 April 2011.
<http://valleyforgemusterrolll.org/encampment.asp>.

April 29th, 2010

12:31:43 p.m. - Investigator - "What colony are you from?"

12:31:51 p.m. - Digital Recorder Response - "Virginia."

12:32:41 p.m. - Digital Recorder Response - "Shannon" - investigators name is being said.

12:32:42 p.m. - EMF Detector - Spikes to caution and then danger, before returning to the safe zone.

12:33:23 p.m. - Digital Recorder Response - "Why?"

12:38:18 p.m. - Investigator - While discussing paranormal activity at another location: "I don't know if you have ever heard about glowing cemeteries, orbs that glow above the cemetery?"

12:38:26 p.m. - Digital Recorder Response - "Yeah."

* Walking toward the National Memorial Arch in the park.

12:45:01 p.m. - Investigator - "Which way should we go?"

12:45:03 p.m. - Digital Recorder Response - "That way!" - female voice.

* Inside a different reconstructed hut in the park.

12:52:32 p.m. - Investigator - "I keep feeling cold air blowing in my face from the top bunk."

12:53:53 p.m. - Investigator - Feels the cold chill again.

The victory of the Continental Army at the end of the American Revolution came at a high cost, but it is doubtful that many would have complained about it. As the Patriot Nathan Hale said before his execution by British troops on September 22, 1776, "I only regret that I have but one life to lose for my country."

Directions: Route 202, near King of Prussia Mall, King of Prussia

Dear Reader:

Thank you for reading *Ghosts and Haunted Places of Pennsylvania*, I truly hope you enjoyed this book and have gained some new insight into the ghosts and spirits that reside in Pennsylvania.

The point of this book, except for a few exceptions, is to introduce places that anyone can investigate. The concessions exist to show some other well-known areas and local haunts. Most of the locations in here close to the public at dark. I must stress this, despite what others may say or do, you can investigate during the day. It is safer, there is no worry about getting caught trespassing, and the ghost still communicate during the day.

As much as we wish we could find peaceful conclusions for all spirits, not every spirit wants to pass on. Sometimes we are only left with the choice to let them be for a future generation. Ghosts can change their minds.

Always keep in mind that many spirits that you come across were once human beings. They are ruled by the same emotions and thoughts that we can be. Let them know that you are there to help them or learn from them, bearing in mind the old saying that you can catch more flies with honey than vinegar. Be respectful and you may be surprised at how conversational the dead can be.

Shannon Boyer Jones

Reference Notes

It is nearly impossible to reference every story, fact, rumor, or account that I have come across over the years but I try to give as much credit as is due. My study of the paranormal has spanned across nearly twenty-years at this point. Through reading books over the years, traveling to these places, field trips in school, friends, co-workers, and so many others who have recounted their tales; there are some points that just cannot be traced back to the original owner. In many cases I have tried and come up empty handed.

Several of the paranormal accounts in this book have come from anonymous accounts by members and acquaintances of the Black Moon Paranormal Society, and the members swear that their accounts are true. Some of the accounts you read may match with other stories that you have heard, these I would say, are the result of the paranormal.

Below I have referenced the quotes, dates, facts, and stories that I have been able to trace.

Locations Visited:

Boiling Springs
Caledonia Iron Furnace
Chickie's Rock
Codorus Iron Furnace
Cornwall Iron Furnace
Fort Hunter
Fort Halifax
Gettysburg
Graeme Park
Grings Mill
Hawk Mountain Sanctuary
Little Buffalo State Park
Lorimer Park
Moonshine Church and Cemetery

Peters Mountain
Pinchot Park
Pine Grove
Valley Forge

Historical Information Gathered on Location at:

Codorus Iron Furnace
Cornwall Iron Furnace
Fort Hunter
Gettysburg National Battlefield
Graeme Park
Hawk Mountain Sanctuary
Little Buffalo State Park
Pine Grove
Valley Forge

Additional Information

Bibliography

Timeline

"Pennsylvania on the Eve of Colonization." *Pennsylvania General Assembly*. 1 Jan. 2011. Web. 1 May 2011.
<www.legis.state.pa.us/wu01/vc/visitor_info/pa_history/pa_history.htm>.

"The Quaker Province: 1681-1776." *Pennsylvania General Assembly*. 1 Jan. 2011. Web. 1 May 2011.
<www.legis.state.pa.us/wu01/vc/visitor_info/pa_history/pa_history.htm>.

Introduction

"The Declaration of Independence." *Independence Hall Association of Pennsylvania*. 4 July. 1995. Web. 20 May. 2011.
<http://www.ushistory.org/declaration/index.htm>.

"Timeline." *Easter State Penitentiary*. 1 Jan. 2011. Web. 20 May 2011.
<www.easternstate.org/learn/timeline>.

"Fort Halifax History." *Fort Halifax Park*. 1 Jan. 2010. Web. 16 May. 2011. <www.forthalifaxpark.org/info.html>.

Avondale Mine

"Avondale Mine Disaster." *Explore PA History*. 1 Jan. 2010. Web. 29 May 2011. <http://explorepahistory.com/hmarker.php?markerid=1-A-ED>.
Pike, C. "Avondale Mine Disaster Site, Plymouth, PA." *Phenomenon and Paranormal Investigations: Truth in Evidence*. 1 Jan. 2011. Web. 29 May 2011. <ppiinvestigations.com/avondale.aspx>.

Belleman's Church Road

"ADALINE BAVER'S GHOST." *Freedom's Corner Haunts & History*. 1 Jan. 2012. Web. 30 Jan. 2012. <https://sites.google.com/site/hauntsandhistory/freedom'scornerhaunts&history>.

Adams III, Charles J. "Was Leesport Apparition the Ghost of Adeline Baver?" The Reading Eagle, 3 Mar. 2010. Web. 1 Jan. 2012. <http://www2.readingeagle.com/article.aspx?id=201392>.

Caledonia Iron Furnace

"Description and Operation." *Iron Furnaces*. Old Industry, 1 Jan. 2011. Web. 15 March 2011. www.oldindustry.org/OH_HTML/OH_Buckeye.html#Description

The Quiet Man. Perf. John Wayne, Maureen O'Hara, Barry Fitzgerald. Republic Pictures, 1952. Film.

Stevens, Thaddeus. "Speech of Mr. Stevens at the Public Meeting in the Court House on Monday, April 10." *Thaddeus Stevens Papers On-line*. Transcribed Cordes Ford. Proof. Brad Burgess. Furman University, 10 Apr. 1865. Web. 10 Apr. 2011. <http://history.furman.edu/benson/hst41/red/stevens3.htm>.

Washlaski, Raymond A., and Ryan A. Washlaski. "Caledonia Furnace Caledonia Forge." *Pa Iron Works*. Rootsweb.ancestry, 1 Jan. 2002. Web. 19 Apr. 2011. <http://paironworks.rootsweb.ancestry.com/fracaledonia.html>.

Boiling Springs

"Boiling Springs." *Boiling Springs*. 1 Jan. 2012. Web. 10 Mar. 2012. <www.boilingsprings.org>.

Chickies Rock

Gulley, Rosemary Ellen. "Chickies Rock." *Ghost Hunting Pennsylvania*. Birmingham: Clerisy, 2009. 129. Print.

"History." *Penn's Cave and Wildlife Park*. 1 Jan. 2011. Web. 12 Apr. 2011. <www.pennscave.com/history.php>.

Nesbitt, Mark, and Patty A. Wilson. "The Ghostly Screams of Chickies Rock." *The Big Book of Pennsylvania Ghost Stories*. Stackpole, 2008. 116-119. Print.

Codorus Furnace

"Codorus Furnace." *Hellam Township*. 1 Jan. 2011. Web. 31 Mar. 2011. <http://www.hellamtownship.com/index.asp?Type=B_BASIC&SEC=%7B1432E3D0-BDBF-45F8-9543-4CA759619B4C%7D>.

Colebrook Furnace

Asfar, Dan. "The Hounds of Colebrook Furnace." *Ghost Stories of Pennsylvania*. Lone Pine International, 2002. 172-182. Print.

Fort Hunter

Dickson, Carl A. *Fort Hunter Mansion and Park: A Guide*. Mechanicsburg: Stackpole, 2002. 7-32. Print.

Fort Mifflin

"Historic Discovery Made at Fort Mifflin." *11th Pennsylvania Regiment*. 28 Aug.2006.Web.20May. 2011. <http://www.11thpa.org/mifflin_find.html>.

"Fort Mifflin." *Fort Mifflin: The Fort That Saved America*. 1 Jan. 2011. Web. 15 May 2011. <http://fortmifflin.us//about.html>.

"William. Howe of Mont. Co. Pa, Executed Fort Mifflin 1864; Info and Descendants." *Howe Family Genealogy Forum*. 10 March. 2008. Web. 20 May 2011. <http://genforum.genealogy.com/howe/messages/4597.html>.

Fort Necessity

"The Battle of Fort Necessity." *National Park Service*. Web. 6 June 2011. <www.nps.gov/fone/battle.htm>.

"The Battle of Monongahela 1755- Braddock's Defeat." *British Battles.* 1 Jan. 2010. Web. 16 May 2011. <www.britishbattles.com/braddock.htm>.

"Fort Necessity: Farmington, Pennsylvania." *Grave Addiction.* 1 Jan. 2011. Web. 1 Jan. 2011. <www.graveaddiction.com/mtwashtav.html7/16/12>.

"The French and Indian War in Pennsylvania." *Explore PA History.* 1 Jan. 2010. Web. 29 May 2011. <http://explorepahistory.com/hmarker.php?markerid=1-A-ED>.

"Mount Washington Tavern, Farmington, Pennsylvania." *Grave Addiction.* 1 Jan. 2011. Web. 1 Jan. 2011. <www.graveaddiction.com/mtwashtav.html7/16/12>.

Washington, George. "Braddock's Defeat, July 18th, 1755." *National Center.* 6 June. 2011. Web. <www.nationalcenter.org/Braddock'sDefeat.html>.

Gettysburg

Brann, James R. "Defense of Little Round Top." *America's Civil War* 1 Nov. 1999. Print.

Coco, Gregory A. *Confederate Killed In Action at Gettysburg.* Gettysburg: Thomas Publications, 2001. Print.

"Kershaw's Brigade at Gettysburg." *Civil War Reference.* 1 Jan. 2011. Web. 2 Apr. 2011. <www.civilwarreference.com/articles/detail.php?article=120>.

"The 20th Maine & 15th Alabama at Little Round Top." *Brother's War.* 2 April. 2011. Web. 2 April. 2011. <http://www.brotherswar.com/Gettysburg-2e.htm>

Graeme Park

"History." *Friends of Graeme Park.* 1 Jan. 2012. Web. 10 Mar. 2012. <www.graemepark.org/>.

Gring's Mill

"Gring's Mill." *Freedom's Corner Haunts & History.* 1 Jan. 2012. Web. 30 Jan. 2012. <https://sites.google.com/site/hauntsandhistory/freedom'scornerhaunts&history4>.
Youker, Darrin. "What's the Story behind Infamous 1875 Murder-suicide? Ask Youker." *The Reading Eagle.*

Http://readingeagle.com/mobile/article.aspx?id=259724., 28 Oct. 2010. Web. 30 Jan. 2012.

Hawk Mountain

"Hawk Mountain Sanctuary." *Freedom's Corner Haunts & History.* 1 Jan. 2012. Web. 30 Jan. 2012. <https://sites.google.com/site/hauntsandhistory/freedom'scornerhaunts&history>.

Huesken Jr., Gerald. "Strange Case of Hawk Mountain and Matthias Schambacher." *Examiner.* 25 Oct. 2010. Web. 30 Jan. 2012. <article/the-strange-case-of-hawk-mountain-and-matthias-schambacher>

Horseshoe Curve

"Altoona, Pennsylvania, Horseshoe Curve Train Wreck February 18, 1947." *Gen Disasters.* 1 Jan. 2011. Web. 18 Apr. 2011. <www.gendisasters.com/data1/pa/trains/altoona-trainwreckfeb1947.htm>.

McIlnay, Dennis. *The Wreck of the Red Arrow: An American Train Tragedy.* Seven Oaks, 2010. Print.

McConnells Mill

"Best Pittsburgh Haunts." *CBS Pittsburgh.* 10 Nov. 2010. Web. 1 June 2011. <http://pittsburgh.cbslocal.com/top-lists/best-pittsburgh-haunts/>.

"McConnells Mills." *Western Pennsylvania Conservancy.* 1 Jan. 2011. 29 July 2012. <www.paconswerve.org/e-conserve/fall-07/30s.htm>

Moonshine Church

"Haunted Moonshine Church and the Blue Eyed Six." *Weird U.S.* 1 Jan. 2012. Web. 29 July 2012. <www.weirdus.com/states/pennsylvania/local_legends/moonshine_church/index.php>.

Pine Grove

Greeley, Horace Andrew. "Recollections, Historical and Otherwise, Relating to Old Pine Grove Furnace." *PATC Archives.* 1 Jan. 2011. Web. 4 May 2011. <www.patc.us/history/archive/pine_grv.html>. A historical reprint from the October 1934 Edition of the Potomac Appalachian Trail Club Bulletin, precursor the PATC's current newsletter, the Potomac Appalachian.

Valley Forge

"The Encampment." *Valley Forge Legacy: The Muster Roll Project.* Friends of Valley Forge, 1 Jan. 2011. Web. 26 April 2011.
<http://valleyforgemusterrolll.org/encampment.asp>.

Photographs

All photographs were taken by me.

Recordings

Archives and Investigations. Black Moon Paranormal Society.
www.blackmoonparanormalsociety.com

ABOUT THE AUTHOR

Shannon Boyer Jones was born and raised in Central Pennsylvania. She obtained a Bachelor of Science degree from Chowan University in 2005, with minors in Psychology and History. In October of 2009 she founded the Black Moon Paranormal Society, where she continues to work as an investigator and researcher.

To contact:

Visit: www.blackmoonparanormalsociety.com

Or find the author on Facebook

Made in the USA
Middletown, DE
07 December 2023

44963836R00073